sew quick
SCRAP QUILTS

Whether you've made one quilt or a hundred, you probably have lots of leftover fabric that you would love to put to good use. With Sew Quick Scrap Quilts, you can fashion all those bits and pieces into wonderful projects. Our handy helpbook features 14 beautiful quilts that can be created using your cherished fabric scraps. And our time-saving techniques enable you to finish traditional patterns — such as Flying Geese, Schoolhouse, Pinwheel, and more — in a short amount of time! So gather your scraps, grab your needle, and enjoy the fun!

LEISURE ARTS, INC.
Little Rock, Arkansas

EDITORIAL STAFF

Vice President and Editor-in-Chief:
  Anne Van Wagner Childs
Executive Director: Sandra Graham Case
Editorial Director: Susan Frantz Wiles
Publications Director: Carla Bentley
Creative Art Director: Gloria Bearden
Senior Graphics Art Director: Melinda Stout

DESIGN
Design Director:
  Patricia Wallenfang Sowers
Senior Designer: Linda Diehl Tiano

PRODUCTION
Senior Publications Editor:
  Sherry Taylor O'Connor
Technical Editors:
  Kathleen Coughran and Beth M. Maher

EDITORIAL
Managing Editor: Linda L. Trimble
Associate Editor: Darla Burdette Kelsay
Assistant Editors:
  Tammi Williamson Bradley and
  Terri Leming Davidson
Copy Editor: Laura Lee Weland

ART
Book/Magazine Graphics Art Director:
  Rhonda Hodge Shelby
Senior Graphics Illustrator:
  Dana Vaughn
Graphics Illustrators: Sonya McFatrich, Keith Melton,
  Mary E. Wilhelm, and M. Katherine Yancey
Photography Stylists: Sondra Daniel,
  Karen Smart Hall, Aurora Huston, and
  Christina Tiano Myers

BUSINESS STAFF

Publisher: Bruce Akin
Vice President, Marketing: Guy A. Crossley
Marketing Manager: Byron L. Taylor
Print Production Manager: Laura Lockhart
Vice President and General Manager:
  Thomas L. Carlisle
Retail Sales Director: Richard Tignor
Vice President, Retail Marketing:
  Pam Stebbins
Retail Marketing Director:
  Margaret Sweetin
Retail Customer Services Manager:
  Carolyn Pruss
General Merchandise Manager: Russ Barnett
Vice President, Finance: Tom Siebenmorgen
Distribution Director: Ed M. Strackbein

Library of Congress Catalog Number 97-73649
International Standard Book Number 1-57486-086-0

TABLE OF CONTENTS

PLEASING

PLAID

Easy enough even for beginners
to create, this handsome spread
is a pleasing combination of plaids
and stripes. Alternating light and
dark values adds interest to the quilt,
and it couldn't be any faster to
finish — simply use embroidery
floss and buttons to tie the layers
into a plush comforter!

Quilter's Rule™ Mini-Square

The **Original** ruler designed by Betty Gall
The only ruler with Fabric Gripping Action.
The lines and numbers are molded into the ruler
for perfect accuracy.

The original ruler designed by a quilter for the craft and quilting enthusiast. Ideal companion for the Rotary Cutter. Simple and easy to use.

How To Use:

1) Place Mini-Square on fabric aligning the straight of grain with one edge of the square. Mark or simply cut around the lower corner of the Mini-Square.
2) Slide Mini-Square to the desired square measurement, aligning with the cut corner. Cut around the top outer edges.

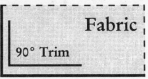

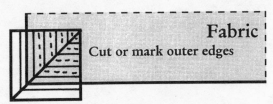

For Bias Squares:

1) Cut strip of fabrics & seam one edge together. Press seam to one side.
2) Align Mini-Square's diagonal line with the seam line of the bias piece.
3) Cut around the lower corner and slide Mini-Square to the desired bias square needed. Cut around outer edges.

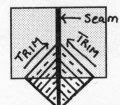

Quilter's Rule International, LLC
817 Mohr Avenue
Waterford, WI   53185 U.S.A.
Telephone: 414/514-2000
Fax: 414/514-2100
E-mail: quilter @ setnet.net

7 32332 10006 5

SKILL LEVEL: 1 2 3 4 5
BLOCK SIZE: 16¹/₂" x 16¹/₂"
QUILT SIZE: 84" x 100"

YARDAGE REQUIREMENTS

Yardage is based on 45"w fabric.

■ 4¹/₄ yds *total* of dark plaids (our quilt uses 11 different dark plaids)

□ 3¹/₂ yds *total* of light plaids and stripes (our quilt uses 9 different light plaids and stripes)
8¹/₂ yds for backing
1 yd for binding
90" x 108" batting

You will also need:
black embroidery floss
20 black 1" buttons

CUTTING OUT THE PIECES

All measurements include a ¹/₄" seam allowance. Follow **Rotary Cutting**, *page 79, to cut fabric.*

1. **From dark plaids:**
   - Cut 46 **strips** 3¹/₄"w.

2. **From light plaids and stripes:** □
   - Cut 20 strips 6"w. From these strips, cut 135 **squares** 6" x 6".

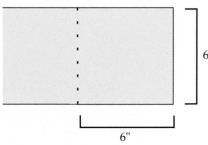

6"

6"

square (cut 135)

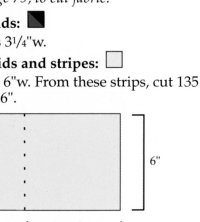

ASSEMBLING THE QUILT TOP

Follow **Piecing and Pressing**, *page 82, to make quilt top. To achieve the scrappy look of our quilt, assemble strips, squares, and units in random fabric combinations.*

1. Sew **strips** together to make **Strip Set A**. Make 23 **Strip Set A's**. Cut across **Strip Set A's** at 3¹/₄" intervals to make **Unit 1**. Make 270 **Unit 1's**.

Strip Set A (make 23)

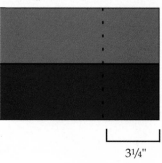

3¹/₄"

Unit 1 (make 270)

2. Sew 2 **Unit 1's** together to make **Unit 2**. Make 135 **Unit 2's**.

Unit 2 (make 135)

6

3. Sew 2 **squares** and 1 **Unit 2** together to make **Unit 3**. Make 45 **Unit 3's**. Sew 2 **Unit 2's** and 1 **square** together to make **Unit 4**. Make 45 **Unit 4's**.

Unit 3 (make 45)

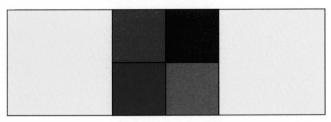

Unit 4 (make 45)

4. Sew 2 **Unit 3's** and 1 **Unit 4** together to make **Block A**. Make 15 **Block A's**. Sew 2 **Unit 4's** and 1 **Unit 3** together to make **Block B**. Make 15 **Block B's**.

Block A (make 15)

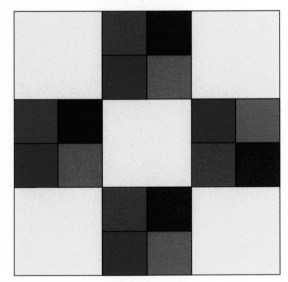

Block B (make 15)

5. Referring to **Quilt Top Diagram**, sew **Blocks** together into rows; sew rows together to complete **Quilt Top**.

COMPLETING THE QUILT

1. Follow **Quilting**, page 87, to layer and tie quilt. Tie quilt at outside corners of **Unit 2's**. Before trimming floss ends, refer to **Quilt Top Diagram** to attach buttons to corners of **Blocks**.
2. Cut a 36" square of binding fabric. Follow **Binding**, page 91, to bind quilt using 2¹/₂"w bias binding with overlapped corners.

Quilt Top Diagram

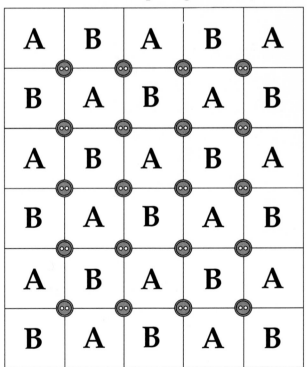

STARRY

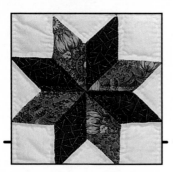

PATH

Precision rotary cutting offers stellar results on our Starry Path quilt, which features a colorful trail of LeMoyne Stars. The radiant spread is ideal for using up fabric scraps, or you can purchase fabrics in a wide assortment of colors and prints to achieve a similar look, such as the cozy coverlet on page 11.

SKILL LEVEL: 1 2 3 4 5
STAR BLOCK SIZE: 6" x 6"
QUILT SIZE: 90" x 108"

YARDAGE REQUIREMENTS
Yardage is based on 45"w fabric.

□ 7³/₄ yds of white solid

▨ 7 yds *total* of assorted prints
8¹/₄ yds for backing
1 yd for binding
120" x 120" batting

CUTTING OUT THE PIECES
All measurements include a ¹/₄" seam allowance. Follow
Rotary Cutting, *page 79, to cut fabric.*

1. **From white solid:** □
   - Cut 29 strips 2¹/₄"w. From these strips, cut 516 **squares** 2¹/₄" x 2¹/₄".
   - Cut 19 strips 3³/₄"w. From these strips, cut 202 squares 3³/₄" x 3³/₄". Cut squares twice diagonally to make 808 **triangles**.
   - Cut 2 lengthwise **side inner borders** 3" x 96¹/₂".
   - Cut 2 lengthwise **top/bottom inner borders** 3" x 83¹/₂".
   - From remaining fabric, cut 20 **large squares** 12¹/₂" x 12¹/₂".

2. **From assorted prints:** ◪
   - Cut 111 strips 1³/₄"w. From these strips, cut 332 **pieces** 1³/₄" x 14".

ASSEMBLING THE QUILT TOP
Follow ***Piecing and Pressing***, *page 82, to make quilt top.*

1. To cut the diamonds for each star, select 2 different print **pieces**. Place **pieces** right sides together, carefully matching raw edges. Referring to **Fig. 1**, align the 45° marking (shown in pink) on the rotary cutting ruler with the lower edge of **pieces**. Cut along right edge of ruler to cut 1 end of the **pieces** at a 45° angle.

Fig. 1

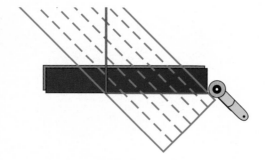

2. Turn cut **pieces** 180° on mat and align the 45° marking on the rotary cutting ruler with the lower edge of the **pieces**. Align the previously cut 45° edge with the 1³/₄" marking on the ruler. Cut at 1³/₄" intervals as shown in **Fig. 2** to cut 4 pairs of **diamonds**.

Fig. 2

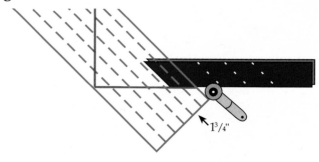

3. Repeat Steps 1 and 2 to cut 166 sets of 4 pairs of **diamonds**. Set aside 38 sets for use in Step 10.

4. Follow **Working with Diamonds and Set-in Seams**, page 84, to sew 1 set of 4 pairs of **diamonds**, 4 **squares**, and 4 **triangles** together to make **Star Block**. Repeat to make 128 **Star Blocks**.

Star Block (make 128)

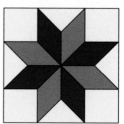

5. Sew 13 **Star Blocks** together to make **Row A**. Make 6 **Row A's**.

Row A (make 6)

6. Sew 2 **Star Blocks** together to make **Unit 1**. Make 25 **Unit 1's**.

Unit 1 (make 25)

7. Sew 5 **Unit 1's** and 4 **large squares** together to make **Row B**. Make 5 **Row B's**.

Row B (make 5)

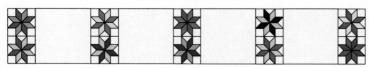

8. Referring to **Quilt Top Diagram**, sew **Row A's** and **Row B's** together to make center section of quilt top.
9. Sew **side**, then **top** and **bottom inner borders** to center section.
10. *(Note:* For Steps 10 - 12, follow **Working with Diamonds and Set-in Seams**, page 84.) Selecting diamonds randomly from those set aside in Step 3, sew 2 **diamonds** and 1 **triangle** together to make **Border Unit**. Make 150 **Border Units**. (You will have 4 diamonds left over.)

Border Unit (make 150)

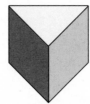

11. Sew 34 **Border Units** and 33 **triangles** together to make **Top/Bottom Pieced Border**. Make 2 **Top/Bottom Pieced Borders**.

Top/Bottom Pieced Border (make 2)

12. Sew 41 **Border Units** and 40 **triangles** together to make **Side Pieced Border**. Make 2 **Side Pieced Borders**.

Side Pieced Border (make 2)

13. Sew **Pieced Borders** to top, bottom, and sides of center section of quilt top, beginning and ending seams exactly 1/4" from each corner of quilt top and backstitching at beginning and end of stitching.

14. Fold 1 corner of quilt top diagonally with right sides together, matching outer edges of borders as shown in **Fig. 3**. Beginning at point where previous seams ended, stitch diamonds together, ending seam 1/4" from edge and backstitching.

Fig. 3

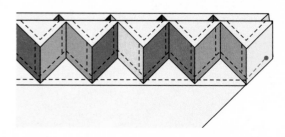

15. Follow Steps 2 - 4 of **Working with Diamonds and Set-in Seams**, page 84, to add **square** to corner where borders are joined.
16. Repeat Steps 14 and 15 with each remaining corner to complete **Quilt Top**.

COMPLETING THE QUILT

1. Follow **Quilting**, page 87, to mark, layer, and quilt using **Quilting Diagram** as a suggestion. Our quilt is hand quilted.
2. Cut a 34" square of binding fabric. Follow **Binding**, page 91, to bind quilt using 2 1/2"w bias binding with mitered corners.

Quilting Diagram

ALBUM

QUILT

Album quilts were introduced during the mid to late 1800's when autograph albums were popular. Pieced from familiar fabrics that stirred memories of loved ones, the quilts were often signed and given as friendship gifts. Our quilt, which is assembled using rotary cutting and unit piecing, was left unsigned to better showcase the pattern.

SKILL LEVEL: 1 2 3 4 5
BLOCK SIZE: 13¹/₂" x 13¹/₂"
QUILT SIZE: 76" x 91"

YARDAGE REQUIREMENTS

Yardage is based on 45"w fabric.

- 3⁵/₈ yds of brown print for block borders
- 3¹/₂ yds of cream solid
- ³/₈ yd *each* of 10 brown prints
  6 yds for backing
  ³/₄ yd for binding
  90" x 108" batting

CUTTING OUT THE PIECES

All measurements include a ¹/₄" seam allowance. Follow Rotary Cutting, page 79, to cut fabric.

1. **From brown print for block borders:**
   - Cut 20 strips 2¹/₄"w. From these strips, cut 60 **side block borders** 2¹/₄" x 10¹/₂".
   - Cut 30 strips 2¹/₄"w. From these strips, cut 60 **top/bottom block borders** 2¹/₄" x 14" and 20 **sashing squares** 2¹/₄" x 2¹/₄".

2. **From cream solid:**
   - Cut 25 strips 2¹/₄"w. From these strips, cut 49 **sashing strips** 2¹/₄" x 14" and 60 **squares** 2¹/₄" x 2¹/₄".
   - Cut 5 strips 2¹/₄"w. From these strips, cut 30 **rectangles** 2¹/₄" x 5³/₄".
   - Cut 9 strips 3³/₄"w. From these strips, cut 90 squares 3³/₄" x 3³/₄". Cut squares twice diagonally to make 360 **side triangles**.
   - Cut 4 strips 2¹/₈"w. From these strips, cut 60 squares 2¹/₈" x 2¹/₈". Cut squares once diagonally to make 120 **corner triangles**.

3. **From *each* brown print:**
   - Cut 2 strips 2¹/₄"w. From these strips, cut 12 **rectangles** 2¹/₄" x 5³/₄".
   - Cut 2 strips 2¹/₄"w. From these strips, cut 24 **squares** 2¹/₄" x 2¹/₄".

ASSEMBLING THE QUILT TOP

Follow Piecing and Pressing, page 82, to make quilt top.

1. Choose 8 matching brown print **squares** and 4 matching brown print **rectangles**. Sew 3 **squares** together to make **Unit 1**. Make 2 **Unit 1's**.

Unit 1 (make 2)

2. Sew 2 **Unit 1's** and 1 **rectangle** together to make **Unit 2**.

Unit 2 (make 1)

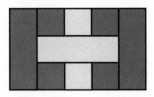

3. Sew 2 **rectangles** and **Unit 2** together to make **Unit 3**.

Unit 3 (make 1)

4. Sew 1 **square**, 2 **side triangles**, and 1 **corner triangle** together to make **Unit 4**. Make 4 **Unit 4's**.

Unit 4 (make 4)

5. Sew 2 **side triangles** and 1 **rectangle** together to make **Unit 5**. Make 2 **Unit 5's**.

Unit 5 (make 2)

6. Sew **Unit 3**, **Unit 5's**, and **Unit 4's** together to make **Unit 6**.

Unit 6 (make 1)

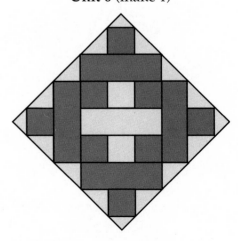

7. Sew 2 **side block borders** and **Unit 6** together to make **Unit 7**.

Unit 7 (make 1)

8. Sew 2 **top/bottom block borders** and **Unit 7** together to make **Block**.
9. Repeat Steps 1 - 8 to make 30 **Blocks**.

Block (make 30)

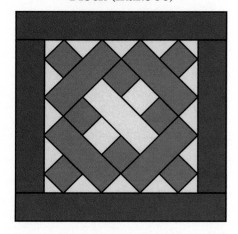

10. Sew 5 **Blocks** and 4 **sashing strips** together to make **Block Row**. Make 6 **Block Rows**.

Block Row (make 6)

11. Sew 5 **sashing strips** and 4 **sashing squares** together to make **Sashing Row**. Make 5 **Sashing Rows**.

Sashing Row (make 5)

12. Referring to **Quilt Top Diagram**, sew **Block Rows** and **Sashing Rows** together to make **Quilt Top**.

COMPLETING THE QUILT

1. Follow **Quilting**, page 87, to mark, layer, and quilt using **Quilting Diagram** as a suggestion. Our quilt is hand quilted.
2. Follow **Binding**, page 91, to bind quilt using 2½"w straight-grain binding with mitered corners.

Quilting Diagram

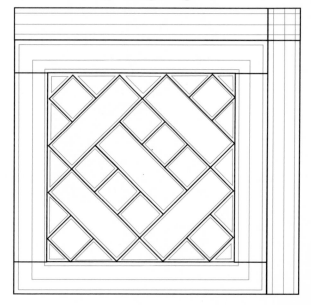

Quilt Top Diagram

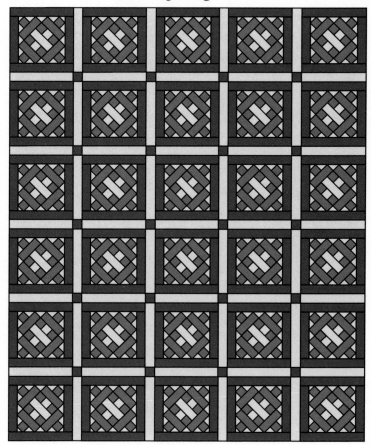

STRING

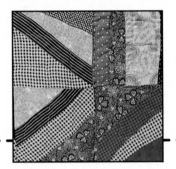

QUILT

This colorful mosaic is reminiscent of quilts made during the Great Depression, when string quilting was introduced. The economical, no-mistakes quilts were pieced from fabrics salvaged from many sources — worn-out clothing, bedding, and even flour sacks! Our simplified version is made by randomly string-piecing scrap fabrics to a muslin square, and we saved even more time by rotary cutting the "strings" to fit after sewing them on!

SKILL LEVEL: 1 2 3 4 5
BLOCK SIZE: 5" x 5"
QUILT SIZE: 71" x 81"

The nature of string quilting is such that different projects may vary greatly in appearance. Our instructions will produce a quilt similar to the antique quilt pictured, but with slightly more uniform pieces.

YARDAGE REQUIREMENTS
Yardage is based on 45"w fabric.

☐ 5³/₈ yds of muslin for foundation squares

■ 7 yds *total* of assorted scrap fabrics
   5 yds for backing
   1 yd for binding
   81" x 96" batting

CUTTING OUT THE PIECES
All measurements include a ¼" seam allowance. Follow **Rotary Cutting***, page 79, to cut fabric.*

1. **From muslin:** ☐
   - Cut 32 strips 5¹/₂"w. From these strips, cut 224 **foundation squares** 5¹/₂" x 5¹/₂".

foundation square (cut 224)

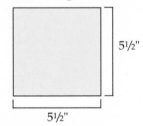

5¹/₂"

5¹/₂"

2. **From scrap fabrics:** ■
   - Cut scrap fabrics into **strips** ("strings") that vary from 1"w to 3"w and are at least 6" long. Strips should have straight edges but may be wider at 1 end than the other.

ASSEMBLING THE QUILT TOP
Follow **Piecing and Pressing***, page 82, to make quilt top.*

1. Place 1 **strip** right side up across center of 1 **foundation square** (**Fig. 1**).

Fig. 1

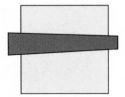

2. Place another **strip** wrong side up on first strip, matching strips along 1 long raw edge. Stitch both strips to foundation square along matched edge. Open second strip and press (**Fig. 2**).

Fig. 2

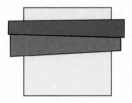

3. Continue adding **strips**, stitching and pressing until foundation square is covered (**Fig. 3**).

Fig. 3

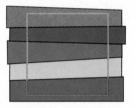

4. Place square on rotary cutting mat with strip-pieced side down. Referring to **Fig. 4**, use rotary cutter and ruler to trim ends of strips even with foundation square to complete **Block**.

Fig. 4

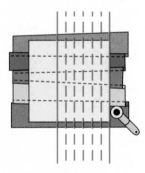

5. Repeat Steps 1 - 4 to make 224 **Blocks**.

Block (make 224)

6. Alternating direction of strips in blocks vertically and horizontally, sew 14 **Blocks** together to make **Row**. Make 16 **Rows**.

Quilting Diagram

Row (make 16)

7. Referring to **Quilt Top Diagram**, sew **Rows** together to complete **Quilt Top**.

COMPLETING THE QUILT
1. Follow **Quilting**, page 87, to mark, layer, and quilt using **Quilting Diagram** as a suggestion. Our quilt is hand quilted.
2. Cut a 36" square of binding fabric. Follow **Binding**, page 91, to bind quilt using 2¹/₂"w bias binding with mitered corners.

Quilt Top Diagram

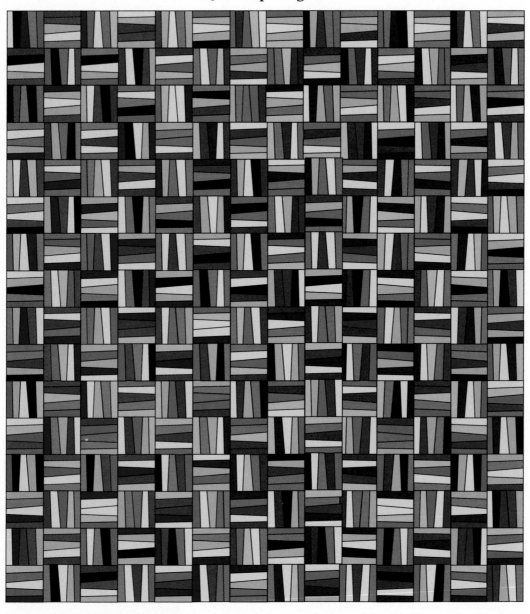

21

SQUARE

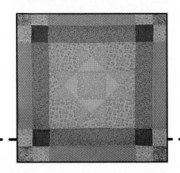

DANCE

Resembling a promenade of dancing calicoes, this Square Dance quilt is pieced using a kaleidoscope of charming prints. Each Ohio Star block is surrounded by a double border and matching sashing strips that create a classic patchwork look. Easy to assemble using rotary cutting shortcuts, the quilt is also shown on page 24 pieced in darker fabrics for a bold, vibrant air.

SKILL LEVEL: 1 2 3 4 5
BLOCK SIZE: 22" x 22"
QUILT SIZE: 97" x 112"

YARDAGE REQUIREMENTS
Yardage is based on 45"w fabric.

■ 12 - 15 yds of assorted scraps
8³⁄₄ yds for backing
1¹⁄₄ yds for binding
120" x 120" batting

CUTTING OUT THE PIECES
All measurements include a ¹⁄₄" seam allowance. Follow Rotary Cutting, page 79, to cut fabric for blocks and sashing.

FOR BLOCKS

1. Study the **Fabric Placement Diagram**, page 28. Each letter in the diagram represents placement for 1 fabric. Choose 8 different scrap fabrics for 1 block and label them A - H.

2. Cut pieces from fabrics as indicated below.

   From Fabric A:
   • Cut 4 **square A's** 4¹⁄₂" x 4¹⁄₂".
   • Cut 1 square 5¹⁄₄" x 5¹⁄₄". Cut square twice diagonally to make 4 **triangle A's**.

   From Fabric B:
   • Cut 1 square 5¹⁄₄" x 5¹⁄₄". Cut square twice diagonally to make 4 **triangle B's**.

   From Fabric C:
   • Cut 1 **square C** 4¹⁄₂" x 4¹⁄₂".
   • Cut 2 squares 5¹⁄₄" x 5¹⁄₄". Cut squares twice diagonally to make 8 **triangle C's**.

   From Fabric D:
   • Cut 4 **strip D's** 3" x 12¹⁄₂".

   From Fabric E:
   • Cut 4 **strip E's** 3" x 12¹⁄₂".

   From Fabric F:
   • Cut 8 **corner square F's** 3" x 3".

   From **Fabric G:**
   • Cut 4 **corner square G's** 3" x 3".

   From Fabric H:
   • Cut 4 **corner square H's** 3" x 3".

3. Label all pieces for block and group into separate stacks.

4. Repeat Steps 1 - 3 to cut fabric pieces for each of 16 blocks in assorted color combinations, using photo as a suggestion. Keep in mind that each fabric may be repeated in another area of a different block – Fabric A in 1 block may be used as Fabric H in another block.

FOR SASHING

1. From assorted scraps:
   • Cut 48 **sashing strips** 3" x 12¹⁄₂".
   • Cut 219 **sashing squares** 3" x 3". (You will need 96 sets of 2 matching squares and 27 unmatched squares.)

ASSEMBLING THE QUILT TOP
Follow Piecing and Pressing, page 82, to make quilt top.

1. Sew 1 **triangle A**, 1 **triangle B**, and 2 **triangle C's** together to make **Unit 1**. Make 4 **Unit 1's**.

Unit 1 (make 4)

2. Sew 2 **square A's** and 1 **Unit 1** together to make **Unit 2**. Make 2 **Unit 2's**.

Unit 2 (make 2)

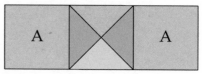

3. Sew 2 **Unit 1's** and 1 **square C** together to make 1 **Unit 3**.

Unit 3 (make 1)

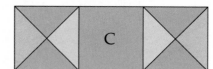

4. Sew **Unit 2's** and **Unit 3** together to make 1 **Unit 4**.

Unit 4 (make 1)

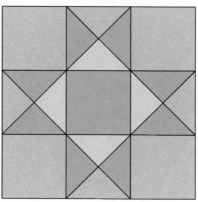

5. Sew 1 **strip D** and 1 **strip E** together to make **Unit 5**. Make 4 **Unit 5's**.

Unit 5 (make 4)

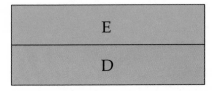

6. Sew 2 **Unit 5's** and **Unit 4** together to make 1 **Unit 6**.

Unit 6 (make 1)

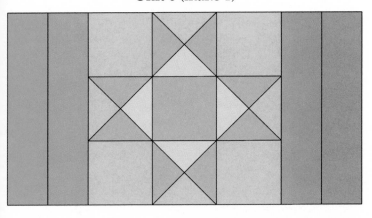

7. Sew 2 **corner square F's**, 1 **corner square G**, and 1 **corner square H** together to make **Unit 7**. Make 4 **Unit 7's**.

Unit 7 (make 4)

8. Sew 2 **Unit 7's** and 1 **Unit 5** together to make **Unit 8**. Make 2 **Unit 8's**.

Unit 8 (make 2)

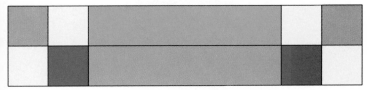

9. Sew **Unit 8's** to top and bottom of **Unit 6** to make **Block**.

Block

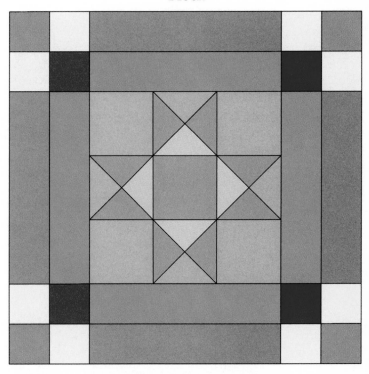

10. Repeat Steps 1 - 9 to make 16 **Blocks**.

11. Sew 2 sets of matching **sashing squares** and 1 **sashing strip** together to make **Sashing Unit**. Make 48 **Sashing Units**.

Sashing Unit (make 48)

12. Sew 4 **Blocks** and 3 **Sashing Units** together to make **Row**. Make 4 **Rows**.

Row (make 4)

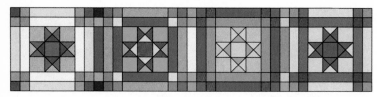

13. Sew 4 **Sashing Units** and 3 **sashing squares** together to make **Sashing Row**. Make 9 **Sashing Rows**.

Sashing Row (make 9)

14. Sew 3 **Sashing Rows** together to make **Sashing Border**. Make 2 **Sashing Borders**.

Sashing Border (make 2)

15. Referring to **Quilt Top Diagram**, sew **Sashing Borders**, **Rows**, and **Sashing Rows** together to complete **Quilt Top**.

COMPLETING THE QUILT
1. Follow **Quilting**, page 87, to mark, layer, and quilt. Our quilt is hand quilted in the ditch along all seamlines.
2. Cut a 34" square of binding fabric. Follow **Binding**, page 91, to bind quilt using 2½"w bias binding with mitered corners.

Fabric Placement Diagram

G	F	E		F	G
F	H	D		H	F
E	D	A	C A C / B / C / A B C / C / A / B C A / C / B A	D	E
F	H	D		H	F
G	F	E		F	G

Each letter in the diagram represents placement for 1 fabric.

FLYING

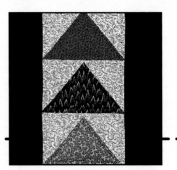

GEESE

Inspired by the majestic formations of migrating snow geese, our version of the Flying Geese pattern uses a fast and extremely accurate paper foundation technique to create the triangle pieces. We simply "punched" the pattern onto sheets of tracing paper using an unthreaded sewing machine and then sewed the fabrics together on the paper foundations.

SKILL LEVEL: 1 2 3 4 5
QUILT SIZE: 95" x 107"

YARDAGE REQUIREMENTS

Yardage is based on 45"w fabric. Due to the nature of paper foundation piecing, yardages given for light print and assorted dark prints are approximate.

- 4³/₈ yds of black solid
- 5 yds of light print
- 4 yds *total* of assorted dark prints
- 2⁵/₈ yds of black print
- ¹/₂ yd of purple solid
  8⁵/₈ yds for backing
  1 yd for binding
  120" x 120" batting

You will also need:
  tracing paper

CUTTING OUT THE BORDERS AND SASHING

All measurements include ¹/₄ " seam allowance. Follow **Rotary Cutting**, *page 79, to cut fabric.*

1. **From black solid:**
   - Cut 7 lengthwise strips 4¹/₄" x 78¹/₂" for **sashing strips**.
   - Cut 2 lengthwise strips 4¹/₄" x 78¹/₂" for **side inner borders**.
   - Cut 2 lengthwise strips 4¹/₄" x 66³/₄" for **top/bottom inner borders**.

2. **From black print:**
   - Cut 2 lengthwise strips 10¹/₂" x 86" for **side outer borders**.
   - Cut 2 lengthwise strips 10¹/₂" x 74¹/₄" for **top/bottom outer borders**.

3. **From purple solid:**
   - Cut 4 **inner border squares** 4¹/₄" x 4¹/₄".
   - Cut 4 **outer border squares** 10¹/₂" x 10¹/₂".

PIECING WITH PAPER FOUNDATIONS

1. Trace **Foundation Pattern**, page 35, onto 1 sheet of tracing paper. Do not cut out.
2. To make foundations, stack up to 12 sheets of tracing paper together and pin traced pattern on top, being careful not to pin over traced lines. Use an unthreaded sewing machine with stitch length set at approximately 8 stitches per inch to "sew" over traced lines of pattern, perforating the paper through all layers. Trim **foundations** to approximately ¹/₄" from outer line. Make a total of 64 **foundations**.

3. Fabric pieces for paper foundation piecing do not have to be cut precisely since they will be trimmed after stitching. To cut pieces for center triangles, "rough cut" a triangle from a dark print ³/₄" - 1" lar than Section 1 on the **foundation**. Triangle should large enough to extend at least ¹/₄" past the section outline when placed right side up over Section 1. C 3 assorted **dark print pieces** to cover a triangle this size.

4. To cut pieces to cover triangles along left edge of foundations, repeat Step 3 to cut 3 **left edge pieces** from light print fabric using Section 2 on the **foundation** as a guide.

5. To cut pieces to cover triangles along right edge of foundations, repeat Step 3 to cut 3 **right edge piece** from light print fabric using Section 3 on the **foundation** as a guide.

6. To secure first fabric piece to foundation, place 1 **da print piece**, right side up, over Section 1 on **foundation**; pin in place (**Fig. 1**).

Fig. 1

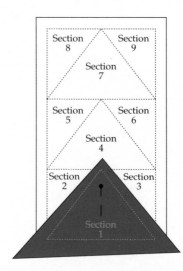

7. To sew left edge piece to foundation, place 1 **left e piece** wrong side up on foundation so that edge of piece extends at least ¹/₄" past line between Section and 2 (**Fig. 2a**). Turn **foundation** over to paper sid and sew pieces together directly on top of line between Sections 1 and 2, extending stitching a few stitches beyond beginning and end of line. Turn to fabric side and trim seam allowances to ¹/₄". Referring to **Fig. 2b**, open out **left edge piece**, pres and pin to **foundation**.

Fig. 2a

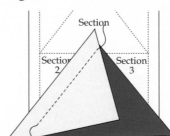

Fig. 2b

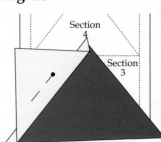

8. To sew right edge piece to foundation, place 1 **right edge piece** wrong side up on **foundation** so that edge of piece extends at least ¼" past line between Sections 1 and 3 (**Fig. 3a**). Turn **foundation** over to paper side and sew pieces together directly on top of line between Sections 1 and 3, extending stitching a few stitches beyond beginning and end of line. Turn to fabric side and trim seam allowances to ¼". Referring to **Fig. 3b**, open out **right edge piece**, press, and pin to **foundation**.

Fig. 3a

Fig. 3b

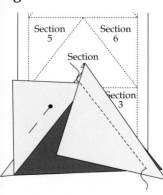
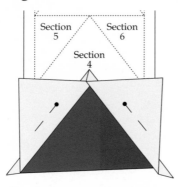

9. Referring to **Foundation Pattern** for sewing sequence, continue sewing **dark print pieces**, **left edge pieces**, and **right edge pieces** to **foundation** until foundation is completely covered.
10. To complete **Flying Geese Unit**, trim fabric and foundation ¼" from outermost lines. Carefully tear away **foundation**.

Flying Geese Unit

11. Repeat Steps 3 - 10 to make a total of 64 **Flying Geese Units**.

ASSEMBLING THE QUILT TOP

*Follow **Piecing and Pressing**, page 82, to make quilt top.*

1. Sew 8 **Flying Geese Units** together to make **Flying Geese Strip**. Make 8 **Flying Geese Strips**.

Flying Geese Strip (make 8)

2. Referring to **Quilt Top Diagram**, page 34, sew **Flying Geese Strips** and **sashing strips** together to make center section of quilt top.
3. Sew 1 **inner border square** to each end of each **side inner border**. Sew **top**, **bottom**, then **side inner borders** to center section.
4. Sew 1 **outer border square** to each end of each **side outer border**. Sew **top**, **bottom**, then **side outer borders** to center section to complete **Quilt Top**.

COMPLETING THE QUILT

1. Follow **Quilting**, page 87, to mark, layer, and quilt using Quilting Diagram as a suggestion. Our quilt is hand quilted using clamshell, cable, feather wreath, and heart designs.
2. Cut a 34" square of binding fabric. Follow **Binding**, page 91 to bind quilt using 2½"w bias binding with mitered corners.

Quilting Diagram

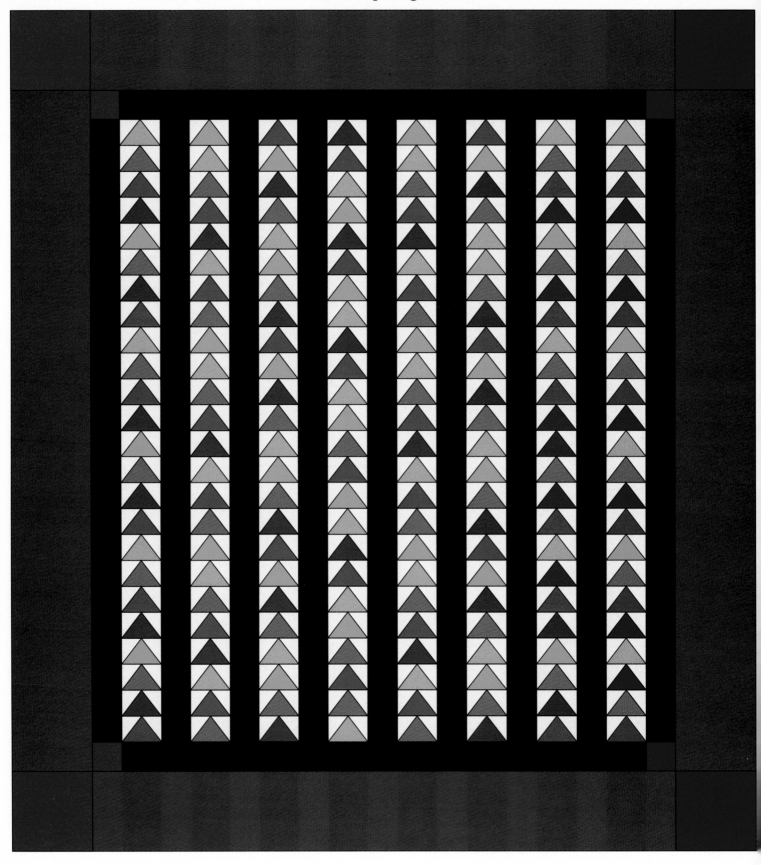

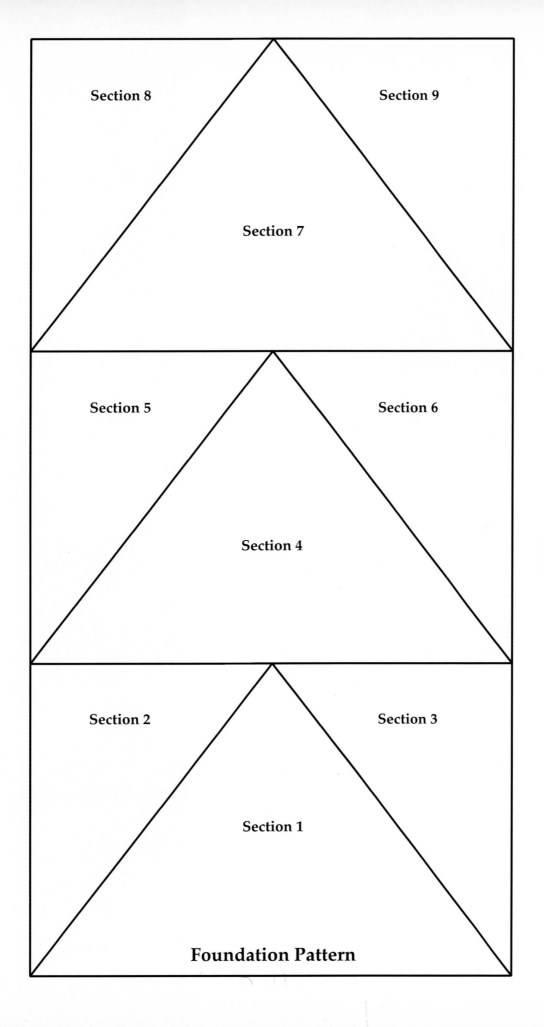

Section 8

Section 9

Section 7

Section 5

Section 6

Section 4

Section 2

Section 3

Section 1

Foundation Pattern

PINWHEEL

QUILT

*F*avorite playthings for generations, swirling, twirling pinwheels were the inspiration for the fun-loving pattern featured on this quilt. Pieced with one main color and an assortment of dark and light prints or plaids, the quilt is one of the easier versions of the Pinwheel pattern.

SKILL LEVEL: 1 2 **3** 4 5
BLOCK SIZE: 13" x 13"
QUILT SIZE: 76" x 92"

YARDAGE REQUIREMENTS

Yardage is based on 45"w fabric.

- ◼ 3⅞ yds of dark red solid
- ◼ 1 fat quarter (18" x 22" piece) *each* of 15 dark prints and/or plaids
- ◻ 1 fat quarter (18" x 22" piece) *each* of 15 light prints and/or plaids
- ◼ ¼ yd of blue print
  6⅛ yds for backing
  1 yd for binding
  90" x 108" batting

CUTTING OUT THE PIECES

All measurements include a ¼" seam allowance. Follow Rotary Cutting, page 79, to cut fabric.

1. **From dark red solid:** ◼
   - Cut 40 strips 3"w. From these strips, cut 79 **sashing strips** 3" x 13½".
   - From pieces of strips remaining, cut 60 **rectangles** 3" x 5¾".
2. **From dark prints/plaids:** ◼
   - Cut *each* fat quarter into 2 **rectangles** 11" x 18" for triangle-squares.
3. **From light prints/plaids:** ◻
   - Cut *each* fat quarter into 2 **rectangles** 11" x 18" for triangle-squares.
4. **From blue print:** ◼
   - Cut 2 strips 3"w. From these strips, cut 20 **sashing squares** 3" x 3".

ASSEMBLING THE QUILT TOP

Follow Piecing and Pressing, page 82, to make quilt top.

1. To make triangle-squares, place 1 light and 1 dark **rectangle** right sides together. Referring to **Fig. 1**, follow **Making Triangle-Squares**, page 83, to make 16 **triangle-squares**. Repeat with remaining **rectangles** to make a total of 480 **triangle-squares**.

Fig. 1

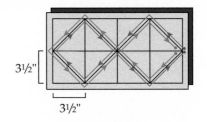

triangle-square (make 480)

2. Sew 4 matching **triangle-squares** together to make **Unit 1**. Make 120 **Unit 1's**.

Unit 1 (make 120)

3. Combining units in random color order, sew 2 **Unit 1's** and 1 **rectangle** together to make **Unit 2**. Make 60 **Unit 2's**.

Unit 2 (make 60)

4. Sew 2 **Unit 2's** and 1 **sashing strip** together to make **Block**. Make 30 **Blocks**.

Block (make 30)

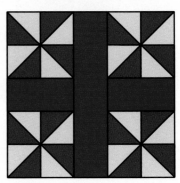

Quilting Diagram

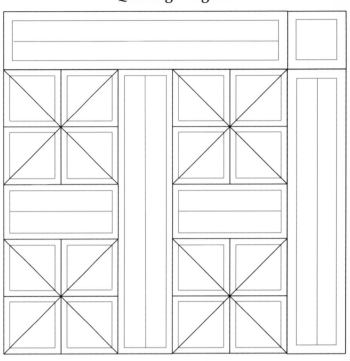

5. Sew 5 **Blocks** and 4 **sashing strips** together to make **Block Row**. Make 6 **Block Rows**.

Block Row (make 6)

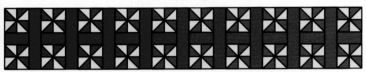

6. Sew 5 **sashing strips** and 4 **sashing squares** together to make **Sashing Row**. Make 5 **Sashing Rows**.

Sashing Row (make 5)

7. Referring to **Quilt Top Diagram**, sew **Block Rows** and **Sashing Rows** together to make **Quilt Top**.

COMPLETING THE QUILT

1. Follow **Quilting**, page 87, to mark, layer, and quilt using **Quilting Diagram** as a suggestion. Our quilt is hand quilted.
2. Cut a 32" square of binding fabric. Follow **Binding**, page 91, to bind quilt using 2¹/₂"w bias binding with mitered corners.

Quilt Top Diagram

PRAIRIE

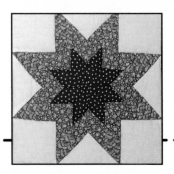

STARS

Our Prairie Stars quilt shines
with the country style of eight-pointed
star motifs that are created using
a scaled-down version of the majestic
Lone Star pattern. To simplify each
block, we used strip-pieced sets to cut
the diamond pieces with accuracy
and ease. The result is a dazzling
arrangement of blocks set in straight
rows with simple sashing.

SKILL LEVEL: 1 2 3 4 5
BLOCK SIZE: 12" x 12"
QUILT SIZE: 92" x 106"

YARDAGE REQUIREMENTS

Yardage is based on 45"w fabric.

- 4 yds of red print for sashing and inner borders
- 3½ yds *total* of assorted blue prints
- 3½ yds *total* of assorted red prints
- 3⅜ yds of blue print for outer borders
- 2½ yds of white solid
  8⅜ yds for backing
  1 yd for binding
  120" x 120" batting

CUTTING OUT THE PIECES

All measurements include a ¼" seam allowance. Follow Rotary Cutting, page 79, to cut fabric.

1. **From red print for sashing and inner borders:**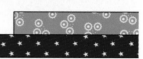
   - Cut 9 strips 2½"w. From these strips, cut 25 **short sashing strips** 2½" x 12½".
   - Cut 2 lengthwise **side inner borders** 2½" x 109".
   - Cut 2 lengthwise **top/bottom inner borders** 2½" x 95".
   - Cut 4 lengthwise **long sashing strips** 2½" x 82½".

2. **From assorted blue prints:**
   - For *each* of 15 **Block A's**, cut 2 *different* **strips** 1¾"w.
   - For *each* of 15 **Block B's**, cut 2 *matching* **strips** 1¾"w.

3. **From assorted red prints:**
   - For *each* of 15 **Block A's**, cut 2 *matching* **strips** 1¾"w.
   - For *each* of 15 **Block B's**, cut 2 *different* **strips** 1¾"w.

4. **From blue print for outer borders:**
   - Cut 2 lengthwise **side outer borders** 10" x 109".
   - Cut 2 lengthwise **top/bottom outer borders** 10" x 95".

5. **From white solid:**
   - Cut 12 strips 4"w. From these strips, cut 120 **squares** 4" x 4".
   - Cut 5 strips 6¼"w. From these strips, cut 30 squares 6¼" x 6¼". Cut squares twice diagonally to make 120 **triangles**.

ASSEMBLING THE QUILT TOP

Follow Piecing and Pressing, page 82, to make quilt top.

1. For Block A, choose 2 *different* blue print **strips** and matching red print **strips**. Sew **strips** together, adding each blue print **strip** 1¾" from the end of red print **strip** to make **Strip Sets A** and **B**.

Strip Set A (make 1)

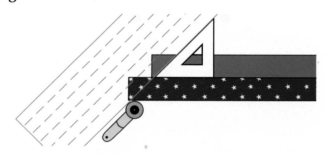

Strip Set B (make 1)

2. Referring to **Fig. 1**, use a large right-angle triangle aligned with the seam to determine an accurate 45° cutting line. Use rotary cutter and rotary cutting rul to trim uneven ends from one end of **Strip Set A** an **Strip Set B**.

Fig. 1

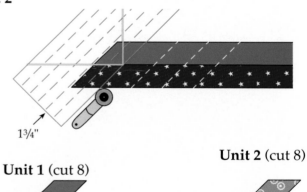

3. Aligning the 45° mark (shown in yellow) on the rotary cutting ruler with a seam and aligning the 1¾" mark with cut edge made in Step 2, cut across **Strip Sets** at 1¾" intervals as shown in **Fig. 2** to cut **Unit 1's** from **Strip Set A** and 8 **Unit 2's** from **Strip Set B**.

Fig. 2

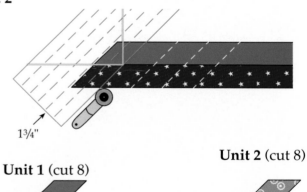

1¾"

Unit 1 (cut 8)

Unit 2 (cut 8)

4. When making **Unit 3's**, refer to **Fig. 3** to match long edges of units. Seams will cross 1/4" from cut edges of fabric. Pin and stitch as shown in **Fig. 3**. Sew 1 **Unit 1** and 1 **Unit 2** together to make **Unit 3**. Make 8 **Unit 3's**.

Fig. 3

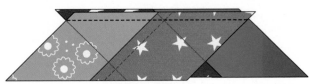

Unit 3 (make 8)

5. To make **Unit 4**, place 2 **Unit 3's** right sides together, carefully matching edges and seams; pin. Stitch in direction shown in **Fig. 4**, ending stitching 1/4" from edge of fabric (you may find it helpful to mark a small dot at this point before sewing) and backstitching at end of seam. Make 4 **Unit 4's**.

Fig. 4   **Unit 4** (make 4)

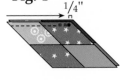 

6. Sew **Unit 4's** together to make **Star**, ending stitching 1/4" from outer edges and backstitching at end of each seam.

Star

7. Follow Steps 2 - 4 of **Working with Diamonds and Set-in Seams**, page 84, to sew **triangles**, then **squares** to **Star** to make **Block A**.

Block A

8. Repeat Steps 1 - 7 to make 15 **Block A's**.
9. For Block B, choose 2 *different* red print **strips** and 2 *matching* blue print **strips**. Sew **strips** together, adding each red print **strip** 1 3/4" from the end of blue print **strip** to make **Strip Sets C** and **D**.

Strip Set C (make 1)

Strip Set D (make 1)

10. Repeat Steps 2 and 3 to cut 8 **Unit 5's** from **Strip Set C** and 8 **Unit 6's** from **Strip Set D**.

Unit 5 (cut 8)   **Unit 6** (cut 8)

11. Referring to **Block B** diagram, repeat Steps 4 - 7 to make **Block B**.

Block B

12. Repeat Steps 9 - 11 to make 15 **Block B's**.

13. Referring to **Quilt Top Diagram** and alternating **Block A's** and **Block B's**, sew 6 **Blocks** and 5 **short sashing strips** together to make vertical **Row**. Make 5 vertical **Rows**. Sew **Rows** and **long sashing strips** together to make center section of quilt top.

14. Sew **borders** together to make **Border Unit**. Make 2 **Side Border Units** and 2 **Top/Bottom Border Units**.

Border Unit

15. Follow **Adding Mitered Borders**, page 86, to attach **Top/Bottom Border Units** and **Side Border Units** to center section to complete **Quilt Top**.

COMPLETING THE QUILT

1. Follow **Quilting**, page 87, to mark, layer, and quilt using **Quilting Diagram** as a suggestion. Our quilt is hand quilted.

2. Cut a 33" square of binding fabric. Follow **Binding**, page 91, to bind quilt using 2¹/₂"w bias binding with mitered corners.

Quilting Diagram

BROKEN

DISHES

Popular across America in the early 1800's, the Broken Dishes pattern has always been a favorite way to use up a variety of scrap fabrics. Created with four triangle-squares, each Broken Dishes block is simple enough for even a beginner to create. Our instructions show you how to use a special ruler to quickly rotary cut accurate triangles with ease.

SKILL LEVEL: 1 2 3 4 5
BLOCK SIZE: 6½" x 6½"
QUILT SIZE: 72" x 85"

YARDAGE REQUIREMENTS

Yardage is based on 45"w fabric.

- 2¾ yds of dark red print
- 4 - 5 yds of assorted dark print scraps
- 4 - 5 yds of assorted light print scraps
  5¼ yds for backing
  1 yd for binding
  81" x 96" batting

You will also need:
  Easy Angle™ Rotary Cutting Ruler (made by EZ International)

CUTTING OUT THE BORDERS

All measurements include a ¼" seam allowance. Follow Rotary Cutting, page 79, to cut fabric.

1. **From dark red print:**
   - Cut 2 lengthwise strips 3¼" x 69" for **top/bottom borders**.
   - Cut 2 lengthwise strips 3¼" x 88" for **side borders**.

CUTTING OUT THE TRIANGLES

1. To cut triangles, refer to **Fig. 1** to line up left edge of Easy Angle ruler with straight grain of 1 fabric scrap. Cut along bottom and left edges of ruler.

Fig. 1

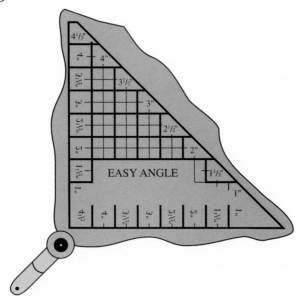

2. Referring to **Fig. 2**, line up bottom edge of ruler with bottom cut edge of fabric; slide ruler to left until 3¾" line (shown in pink) is aligned with left cut edge of fabric. Cut along angled edge of ruler to complete **triangle**.

Fig. 2

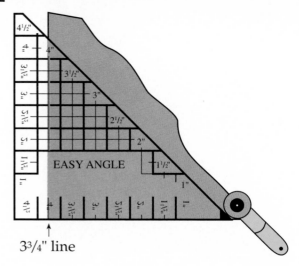

↑
3¾" line

3. Repeat Steps 1 and 2 with remaining scraps to make a total of 480 **dark triangles** and 480 **light triangles**.

dark triangle (cut 480)   **light triangle** (cut 480)

 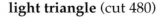

ASSEMBLING THE QUILT TOP

Follow Piecing and Pressing, page 82, to make quilt top.

1. Sew 1 **dark** and 1 **light triangle** together to make **triangle-square**. Make 480 **triangle-squares**.

triangle-square (make 480)

2. Sew 4 **triangle-squares** together to make **Block**. Make 120 **Blocks**.

Block (make 120)

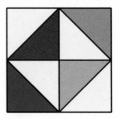

3. Sew 10 **Blocks** together to make **Row**. Make 12 **Rows**.

Row (make 12)

4. Referring to **Quilt Top Diagram**, sew **Rows** together to make center section of quilt top.
5. Follow **Adding Squared Borders**, page 86, to sew **top**, **bottom**, then **side borders** to center section to complete **Quilt Top**.

COMPLETING THE QUILT

1. Follow **Quilting**, page 87, to mark, layer, and quilt. Our quilt is hand quilted in diagonal lines.
2. Cut a 30" square of binding fabric. Follow **Binding**, page 91, to bind quilt using 2¹/₂"w bias binding with mitered corners.

Quilt Top Diagram

SCHOOLHOUSE

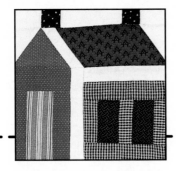

QUILT

Originating in the mid-1800's, the Schoolhouse quilt pattern was inspired by the one-room schools commonly found throughout rural America. Our charming quilt, pieced with homey plaids and ticking, is easy to assemble using unit- and strip-piecing and a few basic templates.

SKILL LEVEL: 1 2 3 4 5
BLOCK SIZE: 9" x 9"
QUILT SIZE: 66" x 87"

YARDAGE REQUIREMENTS

Yardage is based on 45"w fabric.

- 8 yds of assorted scraps
- 2½ yds of cream solid
- 1 yd of blue plaid for sashing
- ⅝ yd *each* of red plaid and tan plaid for sashing
- ¼ yd of black print
  5½ yds for backing
  ⅞ yd for binding
  81" x 96" batting

CUTTING OUT THE PIECES

All measurements include a ¼" seam allowance. Follow **Rotary Cutting**, *page 79, to cut fabric unless otherwise indicated.*

FOR BLOCKS

1. Study the **Fabric Placement Diagram**. Each letter in the diagram represents placement for one fabric. Choose 6 different fabrics for 1 block and label them A - F.
2. Cut pieces from fabrics as indicated below.

   From Fabric A:
   - Cut 2 **long A's** 1½" x 4½".
   - Cut 1 **short A** 1⅞" x 4".
   - Use pattern **A**, page 55, and follow **Template Cutting**, page 81, to cut 1 **triangle A**.

   From Fabric B:
   - Cut 2 **B's** 1½" x 1¾".

   From Fabric C:
   - Use pattern **C**, page 55, and follow **Template Cutting**, page 81, to cut 1 **C**.

   From Fabric D:
   - Cut 2 **D's** 1¾" x 3⅛".

   From Fabric E:
   - Cut 3 **short E's** 1¼" x 3⅛".
   - Cut 2 **long E's** 1½" x 5¼".

   From Fabric F:
   - Cut 1 **F** 2" x 4½".

3. Label all pieces for block and group into separate stacks.
4. Repeat Steps 1 - 3 to cut fabric pieces for each of 48 blocks in assorted color combinations, using photo as a suggestion. Keep in mind that each fabric may be repeated in another area of a different block — Fabric A in 1 block may be used as Fabric F in another block.

5. **From cream solid:**
   - Cut 5 strips 2¼"w. From these strips, cut 96 **G's** 1¾" x 2¼".
   - Cut 3 strips 4"w. From these strips, cut 48 **H's** 1¾" x 4".
   - Cut 2 strips 5¼"w. From these strips, cut 48 **K's** 1¼" x 5¼".
   - Cut 8 strips 1¼"w. From these strips, cut 48 **L's** 5⅞" x 1¼".
   - Use patterns **I** and **J**, page 55, and follow **Template Cutting**, page 81, to cut 96 **I's** (48 in reverse) and 48 **J's**.

Fabric Placement Diagram

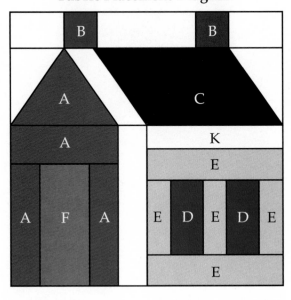

FOR SASHING

1. **From blue plaid:**
   - Cut 14 strips 2"w. From these strips, cut 56 **sashing strips** 9½" x 2".

2. **From red plaid and tan plaid:**
   - From *each* fabric, cut 14 **strips** 1¼"w.

3. **From black print :**
   - Cut 4 strips 2"w. From these strips, cut 63 **sashing squares** 2" x 2".

ASSEMBLING THE QUILT TOP

Follow Piecing and Pressing, page 82, to make quilt top.

1. Sew 2 **G's**, 2 **B's**, and 1 **H** together to make **Unit 1**.

Unit 1

2. Sew 1 **I**, 1 **triangle A**, 1 **J**, 1 **C**, and 1 reverse **I** together to make **Unit 2**.

Unit 2

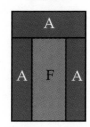

3. Sew 2 **long A's**, 1 **F**, and 1 **short A** together to make **Unit 3**.

Unit 3

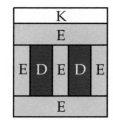

4. Sew 3 **short E's**, 2 **D's**, 2 **long E's**, and 1 **K** together to make **Unit 4**.

Unit 4

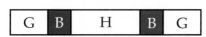

5. Sew **Unit 3**, 1 **L**, and **Unit 4** together to make **Unit 5**.

Unit 5

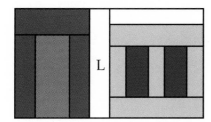

6. Sew **Unit 1**, **Unit 2**, and **Unit 5** together to make **Block**.

Block

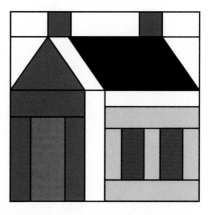

7. Repeat Steps 1 - 6 to make 48 **Blocks**.
8. Sew **strips** together to make **Strip Set**. Make 14 **Strip Sets**. Cut across **Strip Sets** at 9¹/₂" intervals to make 54 **Sashing Units**.

Strip Set (make 14)   **Sashing Unit** (make 54)

9½"

9. Sew 7 **sashing squares** and 6 **Sashing Units** together to make **Sashing Row**. Make 9 **Sashing Rows**.

Sashing Row (make 9)

10. Sew 7 **sashing strips** and 6 **Blocks** together to make **Block Row**. Make 8 **Block Rows**.

Block Row (make 8)

11. Referring to **Quilt Top Diagram**, sew **Sashing Rows** and **Block Rows** together to make **Quilt Top**.

COMPLETING THE QUILT

1. Follow **Quilting**, page 87, to layer and quilt. Our quilt is hand quilted in the ditch along seamlines.
2. Cut a 30" square of binding fabric. Follow **Binding**, page 91, to bind quilt using 2¹/₂"w bias binding with mitered corners.

53

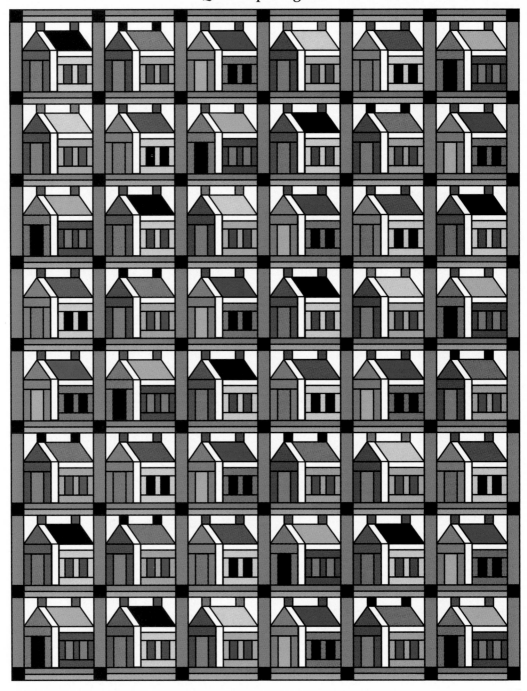

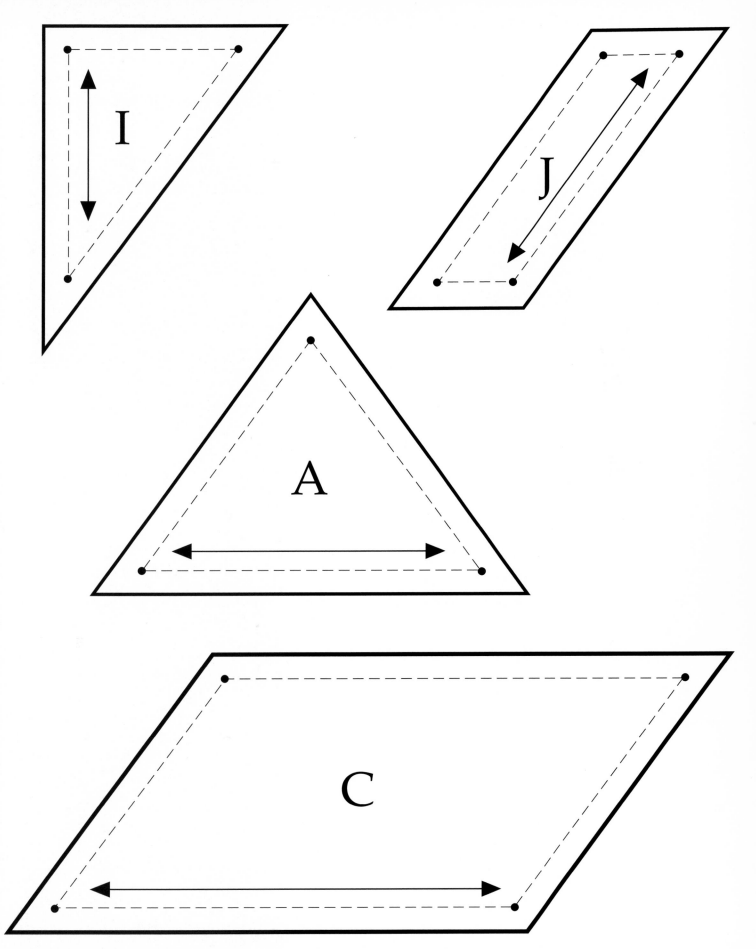

CHURN

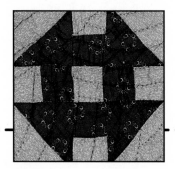

DASH

The classic Churn Dash pattern, with its simple geometric shapes, is reminiscent of the old-time churns that pioneer housewives used to transform fresh milk into sweet, creamy butter. Bringing to mind images of hearth and home, our colorful quilt is pieced in all-American red, white, and blue fabrics with touches of black and tan.

YARDAGE REQUIREMENTS

Yardage is based on 45"w fabric.

- 2⁵/₈ yds of red solid
- 2³/₈ yds of blue print for borders
- ⁷/₈ yd of tan solid
- 1 fat quarter (18" x 22" piece) *each* of 15 light prints
- 1 fat quarter (18" x 22" piece) *each* of 15 dark prints
  5¹/₈ yds for backing
  ³/₄ yd for binding
  81" x 96" batting

CUTTING OUT THE PIECES

All measurements include a ¹/₄ " seam allowance. Follow Rotary Cutting, page 79, to cut fabric.

1. **From red solid:**
   - Cut 18 strips 4¹/₂"w. From these strips, cut 71 **sashing strips** 4¹/₂" x 9¹/₄".

2. **From blue print for borders:**
   - Cut 2 lengthwise **borders** 2¹/₄" x 81".

3. **From tan solid:**
   - Cut 6 strips 4¹/₂"w. From these strips, cut 42 **sashing squares** 4¹/₂" x 4¹/₂".

4. **From *each* light print:**
   - Cut 2 **large squares** 11" x 11" for triangle-squares.
   - Cut 10 **small squares** 2¹/₄" x 2¹/₄".

5. **From *each* dark print:**
   - Cut 2 **large squares** 11" x 11" for triangle-squares.
   - Cut 8 **small squares** 2¹/₄" x 2¹/₄".

ASSEMBLING THE QUILT TOP

Follow Piecing and Pressing, page 82, to make quilt top.

1. To make triangle-squares, place 1 dark and 1 light **large square** right sides together. Referring to **Fig. 1**, follow **Making Triangle-Squares**, page 83, to make 8 **triangle-squares**. Repeat with remaining **large squares** to make a total of 120 **triangle-squares**.

Fig. 1

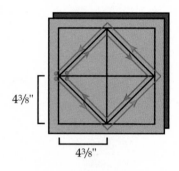

4³/₈"

4³/₈"

triangle-square (make 120)

2. Sew 2 matching **triangle-squares** and 1 each of matching light and dark **small squares** together to make **Unit 1**. Make 2 **Unit 1's**.

Unit 1 (make 2)

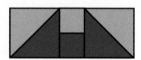

3. Sew 3 light and 2 dark **small squares** together to make 1 **Unit 2**.

Unit 2 (make 1)

4. Sew **Unit 1's** and **Unit 2** together to make **Block**.

Block

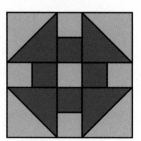

5. Repeat Steps 2 - 4 to make 30 **Blocks**.
6. Sew 6 **sashing strips** and 5 **Blocks** together to make **Block Row**. Make 6 **Block Rows**.

Block Row (make 6)

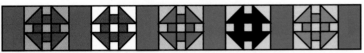

7. Sew 6 **sashing squares** and 5 **sashing strips** together to make **Sashing Row**. Make 7 **Sashing Rows**.

Sashing Row (make 7)

8. Referring to **Quilt Top Diagram**, sew **Sashing Rows** and **Block Rows** together. Sew **borders** to sides to complete **Quilt Top**.

COMPLETING THE QUILT

1. Follow **Quilting**, page 87, to mark, layer, and quilt using **Quilting Diagram** as a suggestion. Our quilt is hand quilted.
2. Follow **Binding**, page 91, to bind quilt using 2¹/₂"w straight-grain binding with overlapped corners.

Quilting Diagram

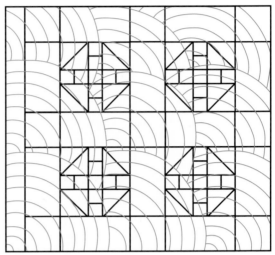

Quilt Top Diagram

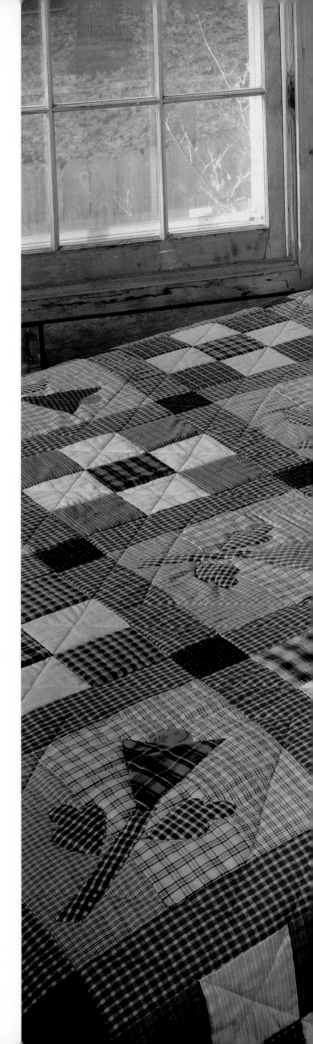

PLAID

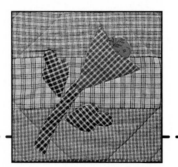

GARDEN

The rustic beauty of homespun plaids is a natural complement to the simple blooms on our Plaid Garden quilt. Each pieced block is made with rotary-cut strip-set units. For no-fuss appliqués, we fused the motifs in place and used clear nylon thread to machine stitch the edges.

YARDAGE REQUIREMENTS
Yardage is based 45"w fabric.

- ■ 4 yds of medium plaid for sashing strips
- ◩ 1⅜ yds *each* of 3 light plaids for background blocks
- ■ ⅞ yd of green plaid for leaf and stem appliqués
- ■ ⅝ yd of dark plaid for sashing squares
- ◻ ½ yd *each* of 3 light plaids for nine-patch blocks
- ◩ ¼ yd *each* of 9 dark plaids for nine-patch blocks
- ◪ ⅛ yd of gold print for flower center appliqués
- ■ scraps of assorted plaids for flower appliqués
  8⅝ yds for backing
  1 yd for binding
  120" x 120" batting

You will also need:
   paper-backed fusible web
   transparent monofilament thread for appliqué

CUTTING OUT THE PIECES
All measurements include a ¼" seam allowance. Follow
Rotary Cutting, page 79, to cut fabric.

1. **From medium plaid for sashing strips:** ■
   - Cut 43 strips 3"w. From these strips, cut 127 **sashing strips** 3" x 11".

2. **From *each* of 3 light plaids for background blocks:** ◩
   - Cut 10 **background strips** 4"w.

3. **From dark plaid for sashing squares:** ■
   - Cut 6 strips 3"w. From these strips, cut 72 **sashing squares** 3" x 3".

4. **From light plaids for nine-patch blocks:** ◻
   - Cut 112 **squares** 4" x 4". You will need 28 sets of 4 matching light plaid squares.

5. **From dark plaids for nine-patch blocks:** ◪
   - Cut 140 **squares** 4" x 4". You will need 28 sets of 1 different and 4 matching dark plaid squares.

PREPARING THE APPLIQUÉS
Use patterns, page 65, and follow Preparing Fusible
Appliqués, page 85, to cut appliqués.

1. **From green plaid for leaf and stem appliqués:**
   - Cut 28 **stems** (12 in reverse).
   - Cut 56 **leaves** (28 in reverse).

2. **From assorted plaids for flower appliqués:**
   - Cut 28 **flowers**.

3. **From gold print for flower center appliqués:**
   - Cut 28 **flower centers**.

ASSEMBLING THE QUILT TOP
Follow Piecing and Pressing, page 82, to make quilt top.

1. Sew 1 set of light plaid **squares** and 1 set of dark plaid **squares** together to make **Nine-Patch Block**. Make 28 **Nine-Patch Blocks**.

Nine-Patch Block (make 28)

2. Sew 3 different **background strips** together to make **Strip Set**. Make 10 **Strip Sets**. Cut across **Strip Sets** at 11" intervals to make 28 **Background Blocks**.

Strip Set (make 10)	**Background Block** (make 28)

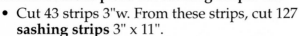
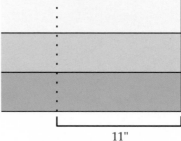
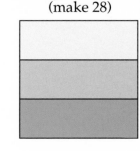

11"

3. Follow **Invisible Appliqué**, page 85, to stitch appliqués to **Background Blocks** to make 12 **Flower Block A's** and 16 **Flower Block B's**.

Flower Block A (make 12)	**Flower Block B** (make 16)

4. Sew 8 **sashing squares** and 7 **sashing strips** together to make **Sashing Row**. Make 9 **Sashing Rows**.

5. Sew 8 **sashing strips**, 4 **Nine-Patch Blocks**, and 3 **Flower Block A's** together to make **Row A**. Make 4 **Row A's**.

6. Sew 8 **sashing strips**, 4 **Flower Block B's**, and 3 **Nine-Patch Blocks** together to make **Row B**. Make 4 **Row B's**.

7. Refer to **Quilt Top Diagram**, page 64, to sew **Sashing Rows**, **Row A's**, and **Row B's** together to complete **Quilt Top**.

COMPLETING THE QUILT

1. Follow **Quilting**, page 87, to mark, layer, and quilt using **Quilting Diagram** as a suggestion. Our quilt is machine quilted.

2. Cut a 34" square of binding fabric. Follow **Binding**, page 91, to bind quilt using 2¹/₂"w straight-grain binding with mitered corners.

Quilting Diagram

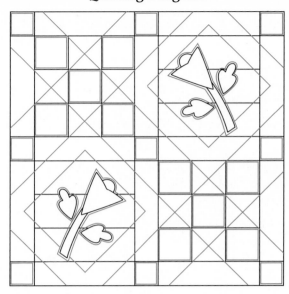

Sashing Row (make 9)

Row A (make 4)

Row B (make 4)

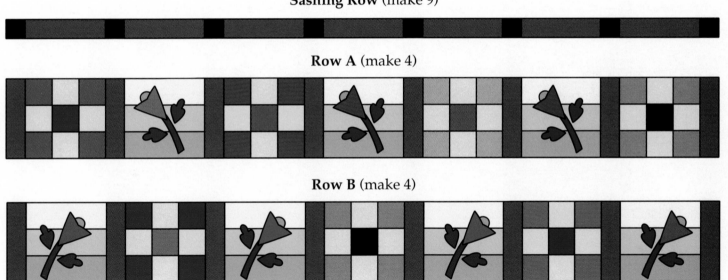

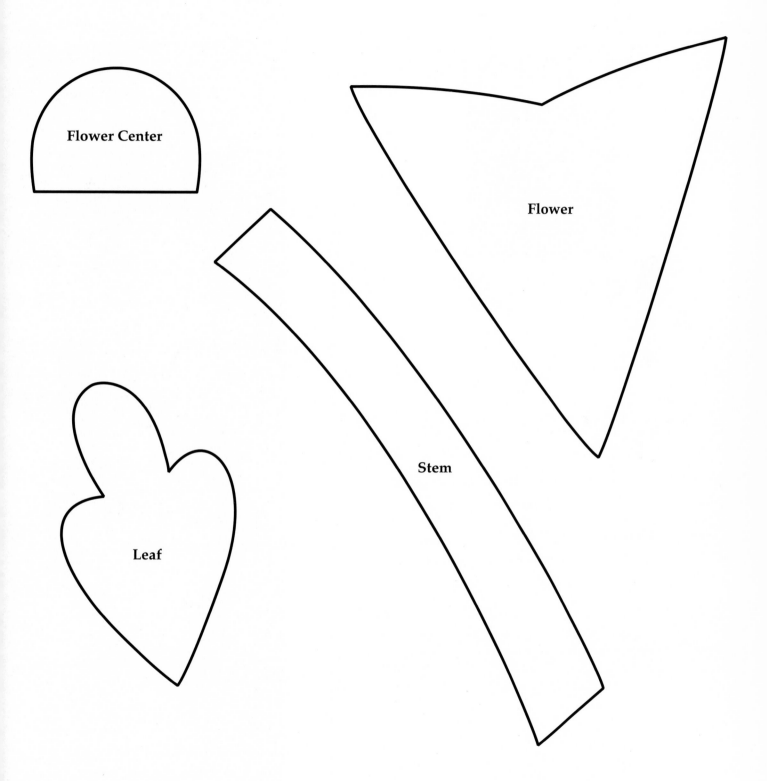

Flower Center

Flower

Stem

Leaf

ROMAN

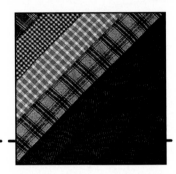

STRIPE

This striking pattern is often called Sunshine and Shadows when pieced in solid fabrics rather than prints. For our Roman Stripe quilt, we selected a variety of rustic plaids for a homespun look and used black for the solid triangles to blend the tones beautifully. To create the striped sections with ease, we rotary cut strip-pieced sets using an angle-cutting ruler.

SKILL LEVEL: 1 2 3 4 5
BLOCK SIZE: 7" x 7"
QUILT SIZE: 78" x 92"

YARDAGE REQUIREMENTS
Yardage is based on 45"w fabric.

- 4⅝ yds of black plaid
- 2¾ yds *total* of assorted plaids
- 2 yds of red plaid
- 1⅞ yds of black solid
  7¼ yds for backing
  1 yd for binding
  90" x 108" batting

You will also need:
   Companion Angle™ Rotary Cutting Ruler (made
      by EZ International)

CUTTING OUT THE PIECES
All measurements include a ¼" seam allowance. Follow
Rotary Cutting, page 79, to cut fabric.

1. **From black plaid:**
   - Cut 2 lengthwise strips 12¼" x 82" for **top/bottom outer borders.**
   - Cut 2 lengthwise strips 12¼" x 72" for **side outer borders.**

2. **From assorted plaids:**
   - Cut a total of 44 **strips** 1¾"w.

3. **From red plaid:**
   - Cut 2 lengthwise strips 2¾" x 67" for **side inner borders.**
   - Cut 2 lengthwise strips 2¾" x 58" for **top/bottom inner borders.**

4. **From black solid:**
   - Cut 7 strips 7⅞"w. From these strips, cut 32 squares 7⅞" x 7⅞". Cut squares once diagonally to make 64 **triangles.** (You will need 63 and have 1 left over.)

square (cut 32)

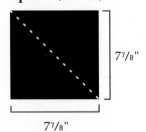

7⅞"

7⅞"

triangle (cut 64)

ASSEMBLING THE QUILT TOP
Follow Piecing and Pressing, page 82, to make quilt top.

1. Sew 4 **strips** together in random color order to make **Strip Set.** Make 11 **Strip Sets.**

Strip Set (make 11)

2. Aligning top and bottom edges of ruler with long edges of strip set, use Companion Angle ruler to cut 63 **Unit 1's** from **Strip Sets,** turning ruler 180° after each cut (**Fig. 1**).

Fig. 1

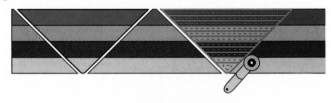

Unit 1 (make 63)

3. Sew 1 **Unit 1** and 1 **triangle** together to make **Block.** Make 63 **Blocks.**

Block (make 63)

4. Sew 7 **Blocks** together to make **Row.** Make 9 **Rows.**

Row (make 9)

5. Referring to **Quilt Top Diagram**, sew **Rows** together to make center section of quilt top.
6. Follow **Adding Squared Borders**, page 86, to sew **side**, then **top** and **bottom inner borders** to center section. Add **side**, then **top** and **bottom outer borders** to complete **Quilt Top**.

COMPLETING THE QUILT

1. Follow **Quilting**, page 87, to mark, layer, and quilt using **Quilting Diagram** as a suggestion. Our quilt is machine quilted.
2. Cut a 34" square of binding fabric. Follow **Binding**, page 91, to bind quilt using 2¹/₂"w bias binding with mitered corners.

Quilting Diagram

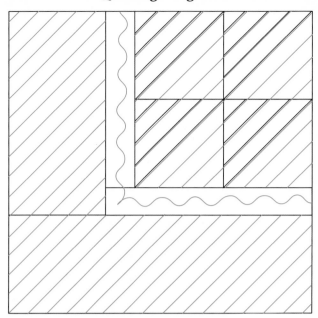

Quilt Top Diagram

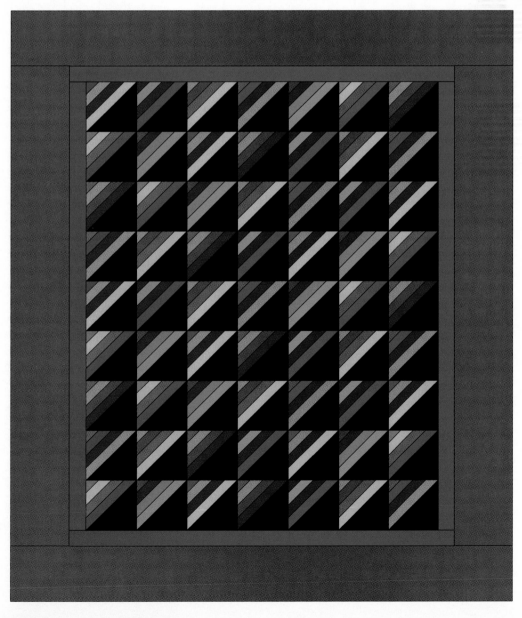

PINEAPPLE

QUILT

The pattern in this Log Cabin variation represents a traditional Colonial symbol of hospitality — the pineapple. Log Cabin quilts are known for their simplicity, and we eliminated a step to make our version even easier. Instead of stitching on a foundation block, we pieced the fabric strips around a center square and rotary cut them into shape.

YARDAGE REQUIREMENTS

Yardage is based on 45"w fabric.

■ 10 yds *total* of assorted dark prints

□ 6 yds *total* of assorted light prints
8¼ yds for backing
1 yd for binding
120" x 120" batting

You will also need:
12½" x 12½" square rotary cutting ruler

CUTTING OUT THE PIECES

All measurements include a ¼" seam allowance. Follow
***Rotary Cutting**, page 79, to cut fabric.*

1. **From assorted dark prints:** ■
    - Cut 142 **strips** 2"w.
    - From remaining fabric, cut 30 **center squares** 3½" x 3½".

2. **From assorted light prints:** □
    - Cut 97 **strips** 2"w.

ASSEMBLING THE QUILT TOP

*Follow **Piecing and Pressing**, page 82, to make quilt top. Assemble blocks in alternating **light** and **dark** rounds, adding strips in random fashion within each round. Use square rotary cutting ruler to align, measure, and cut strips throughout block construction.*

1. For ruler placement guidelines, refer to **Fig. 1** and use a removable marker to precisely mark each **center square** in half horizontally, vertically, and diagonally on the right side of fabric.

Fig. 1

2. (*Note:* For Steps 2 - 7, refer to **Block Diagram**, page 74, and **Table**, page 74, to make block. The **Block Diagram** shows ruler placement guidelines in pink and blue. Use the pink guidelines when adding light rounds and blue guidelines when adding dark rounds. Use the **Table** measurements to align ruler with placement guidelines.) Referring to **Fig. 2**, assemble 1 **center square** and 4 light **strips**, trimming off remainder of each strip after stitching; open and press. Referring to **Fig. 3**, align L1 measurement on ruler with pink placement lines on **center square**. Trim off fabric extending beyond ruler edges. Referring to **Fig. 4**, rotate square ½ turn and repeat for opposite side of square to make **Unit 1**.

Fig. 2

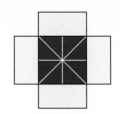

Fig. 3

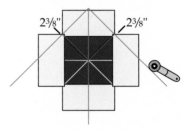

2³/8"   2³/8"

Fig. 4

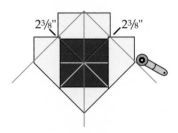

2³/8"   2³/8"

Unit 1

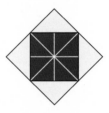

3. Referring to **Fig. 5**, assemble **Unit 1** and 4 dark **strips**, trimming off remainder of each strip after stitching; open and press.

Fig. 5

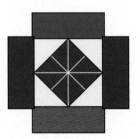

4. Referring to **Fig. 6**, align **D2** measurements on ruler with blue placement lines on **Unit 1**. Cut along ruler edges. Referring to **Fig. 7**, rotate square ¹/₂ turn and repeat for opposite side of square to make **Unit 2**.

Fig. 6

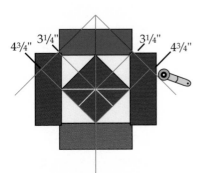

Fig. 7

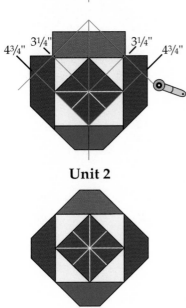

Unit 2

5. Referring to **Fig. 8**, assemble **Unit 2** and 4 light **strips**, trimming off remainder of each strip after stitching; open and press. Referring to **Fig. 9**, align **L3** measurements on ruler with pink placement lines on **Unit 2**. Trim off fabric extending beyond ruler edges. Referring to **Fig. 10**, rotate square ¹/₂ turn and repeat for opposite side of square to make **Unit 3**.

Fig. 8

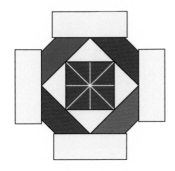

Fig. 9

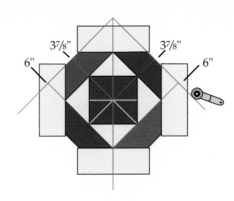

Fig. 10

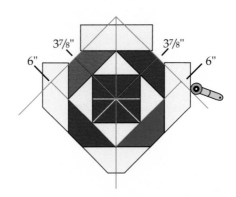

Unit 3

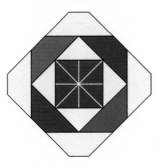

6. Repeat Steps 3 - 5 to add rounds **D4, L5, D6, L7,** and **D8** to make **Unit 4**.

Unit 4

73

7. Add dark **strips** to **Unit 4**. Align **D9** measurements on ruler with blue placement lines on square. Cut 1 corner at a time until all 4 corners are trimmed to make **Unit 5**.

Unit 5

8. Repeat Step 6 to add round **D10** to complete **Block**.

Block

9. Repeat Steps 2 - 8 to make 30 **Blocks**.
10. Referring to **Quilt Top Diagram**, sew 5 **Blocks** together to make **Row**. Make 6 **Rows**. Sew **Rows** together to complete center section of quilt top.
11. Sew 20 **strips** together, alternating light and dark, to make a **Strip Set** 30½"l. Make 3 **Strip Sets**. Cut across **Strip Sets** at 8" intervals to make a total of 14 **Unit 6's**.

Strip Set (make 3)   **Unit 6** (make 14)

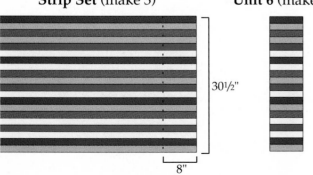

30½"

8"

12. Sew short edges of all **Unit 6's** together to make 1 pieced strip. From this strip, cut 2 **Top/Bottom Border Units** 94"l and 2 **Side Border Units** 109"l.
13. Referring to **Quilt Top Diagram**, follow **Adding Mitered Borders**, page 86, to attach **Top**, **Bottom**, then **Side Border Units** to complete **Quilt Top**.

COMPLETING THE QUILT

1. Follow **Quilting**, page 87, to mark, layer, and quilt using **Quilting Diagram** as a suggestion. Our quilt is hand quilted.
2. Cut a 33" square of binding fabric. Follow **Binding**, page 91, to bind quilt using 2½"w bias binding with mitered corners.

Block Diagram

Table

Round	Light Guideline Measurements (shown in pink)		Dark Guideline Measurements (shown in blue)	
	INSIDE	OUTSIDE	INSIDE	OUTSIDE
L1	$2^{3}/_{8}$"	—		
D2			$3^{1}/_{4}$"	$4^{3}/_{4}$"
L3	$3^{7}/_{8}$"	6"		
D4			$4^{3}/_{4}$"	$6^{1}/_{4}$"
L5	$5^{3}/_{8}$"	$7^{1}/_{2}$"		
D6			$6^{1}/_{4}$"	$7^{3}/_{4}$"
L7	$6^{7}/_{8}$"	9"		
D8			$7^{3}/_{4}$"	$9^{1}/_{4}$"
D9			$7^{3}/_{4}$"	$9^{1}/_{4}$"
D10			$7^{3}/_{4}$"	$9^{1}/_{4}$"

Quilting Diagram

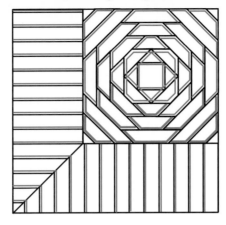

Quilt Top Diagram

GENERAL INSTRUCTIONS

*Complete instructions are given for making each of the quilts shown in this book.
Skill levels indicated for quilts may help you choose the right project. To make your quilting
easier and more enjoyable, we encourage you to carefully read all of these general instructions,
study the color photographs, and familiarize yourself with the individual
project instructions before beginning a project.*

TECHNIQUES

QUILTING SUPPLIES

This list includes all the tools you need for basic quick-method quiltmaking, plus additional supplies used for special techniques. Unless otherwise specified, all items may be found in your favorite fabric store or quilt shop.

Batting — Batting is most commonly available in polyester, cotton, or a polyester/cotton blend (see **Choosing and Preparing the Batting**, page 89).

Cutting mat — A cutting mat is a special mat designed to be used with a rotary cutter. A mat that measures approximately 18" x 24" is a good size for most cutting.

Eraser — A soft white fabric eraser or white art eraser may be used to remove pencil marks from fabric. Do not use a colored eraser, as the dye may discolor fabric.

Iron — An iron with both steam and dry settings and a smooth, clean soleplate is necessary for proper pressing.

Marking tools — There are many different types of marking tools available (see **Marking Quilting Lines**, page 88). A silver quilter's pencil is a good marker for both light and dark fabric.

Masking tape — Two widths of masking tape, 1"w and ¼"w, are helpful to have when quilting. The 1"w tape is used to secure the backing fabric to a flat surface when layering the quilt. The ¼"w tape may be used as a guide when outline quilting.

Needles — Two types of needles are used for hand sewing: *Betweens*, used for quilting, are short and strong for stitching through layered fabric and batting. *Sharps* are longer, thinner needles used for basting and other hand sewing. For *sewing machine needles*, we recommend size 10 to 14 or 70 to 90 universal (sharp-pointed) needles.

Paper-backed fusible web — This iron-on adhesive with paper backing is used to secure fabric cutouts to another fabric when appliquéing. If the cutouts will be stitched in place, purchase the lighter weight web that will not gum up your sewing machine. A heavier weight web is used for appliqués that are fused in place with no stitching.

Permanent fine-point marker — A permanent marker is used to mark templates and stencils and to sign and date quilts. Test marker on fabric to make sure it will not bleed or wash out.

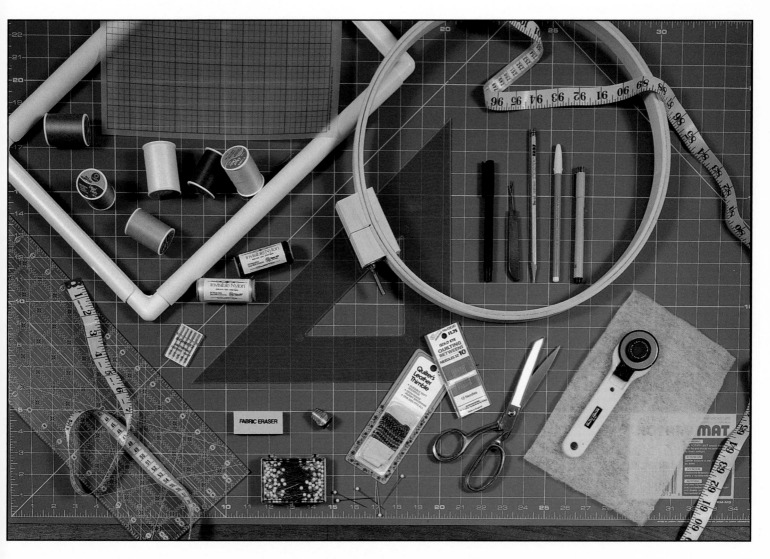

Pins — Straight pins made especially for quilting are extra long with large, round heads. Glass head pins will stand up to occasional contact with a hot iron. Some quilters prefer extra-fine dressmaker's silk pins. If you are machine quilting, you will need a large supply of 1" long (size 01) rust-proof safety pins for pin-basting.

Quilting hoop or frame — Quilting hoops and frames are designed to securely hold the 3 layers of a quilt together while you quilt. Many different types and sizes are available, including round and oval wooden hoops, frames made of rigid plastic pipe, and large floor frames made of either material. A 14" or 16" hoop allows you to quilt in your lap and makes your quilting portable.

Rotary cutter — The rotary cutter is the essential tool for quick-method quilting techniques. The cutter consists of a round, sharp blade mounted on a handle with a retractable blade guard for safety. It should be used only with a cutting mat and rotary cutting ruler. Two sizes are generally available; we recommend the larger (45 mm) size.

Rotary cutting rulers — A rotary cutting ruler is a thick, clear acrylic ruler made specifically for use with a rotary cutter. It should have accurate $1/8$" crosswise and lengthwise markings and markings for 45° and 60° angles. A 6" x 24" ruler is a good size for most cutting. An additional 6" x 12" ruler or $12^{1}/_{2}$" square ruler is helpful when cutting wider pieces. Many specialty rulers are available that make specific cutting tasks faster and easier.

Scissors — Although most cutting will be done with a rotary cutter, sharp, high-quality scissors are still needed for some cutting. A separate pair of scissors for cutting paper and plastic is recommended. Smaller scissors are handy for clipping threads.

Seam ripper — A good seam ripper with a fine point is useful for removing stitching.

Sewing machine — A sewing machine that produces a good, even straight stitch is all that is necessary for most quilting. Zigzag stitch capability is necessary for Invisible Appliqué. Clean and oil your machine often and keep the tension set properly.

Stabilizer — Commercially made non-woven material or paper stabilizer is placed behind background fabric when doing Invisible Appliqué to provide a more stable stitching surface.

Tape measure — A flexible 120" long tape measure is helpful for measuring a quilt top before adding borders.

Template material — Sheets of translucent plastic, often pre-marked with a grid, are made especially for making templates and quilting stencils.

Thimble — A thimble is necessary when hand quilting. Thimbles are available in metal, plastic, or leather and in many sizes and styles. Choose a thimble that fits well and is comfortable.

Thread — Several types of thread are used for quiltmaking: *General-purpose* sewing thread is used for basting, piecing, and some appliquéing. Buy high-quality cotton or cotton-covered polyester thread in light and dark neutrals, such as ecru and grey, for your basic supplies. *Quilting* thread is stronger than general-purpose sewing thread, and some brands have a coating to make them slide more easily through the quilt layers. Some machine appliqué projects in this book use *transparent monofilament* (clear nylon) thread. Use a very fine (.004 mm), soft nylon thread that is not stiff or wiry. Choose clear nylon thread for white or light fabrics or smoke nylon thread for darker fabrics.

Triangle — A large plastic right-angle triangle (available in art and office supply stores) is useful in rotary cutting for making first cuts to "square up" raw edges of fabric and for checking to see that cuts remain at right angles to the fold.

Walking foot — A walking foot or even-feed foot is needed for straight-line machine quilting. This special foot will help all 3 layers of the quilt move at the same rate over the feed dogs to provide a smoother quilted project.

FABRICS

SELECTING FABRICS

For many quilters, choosing fabrics for a new quilt project is one of the most fun, yet most challenging, parts of quiltmaking. Photographs of our quilts are excellent guides for choosing the colors for your quilt. You may choose to duplicate the colors in the photograph, or you may use the same light, medium, and dark values in completely different color families. When you change the light and dark value placement in a quilt block, you may come up with a surprising new creation. The most important lesson to learn about fabrics and color is to choose fabrics you love. When you combine several fabrics you are simply crazy about in a quilt, you are sure to be happy with the results!

The yardage requirements listed for each project are based on 45" wide fabric with a "usable" width of 42" after shrinkage and trimming selvages. Your actual usable width will probably vary slightly from fabric to fabric. Though most fabrics will yield 42" or more, if you find a fabric that you suspect will yield a narrower usable width you will need to purchase additional yardage to compensate. Our recommended yardage lengths should be adequate for occasional resquaring of fabric when many cuts are required, but it never hurts to buy a little more fabric for insurance against a narrower usable width, the occasional cutting error, or to have on hand for making coordinating projects.

Choose high-quality, medium-weight, 100% cotton fabrics such as broadcloth or calico. All-cotton fabrics hold a crease better, fray less, and are easier to quilt than cotton/polyester blends. All the fabrics for a quilt should be of comparable weight and weave. Check the end of the fabric bolt for fiber content and width.

PREPARING FABRICS

All fabrics should be washed, dried, and pressed before cutting.

1. To check colorfastness before washing, cut a small piece of the fabric and place in a glass of hot water with a little detergent. Leave fabric in the water for a few minutes. Remove from water and blot fabric with white paper towels. If any color bleeds onto the towels, wash the fabric separately with warm water and detergent, then rinse until the water runs clear. If fabric continues to bleed, choose another fabric.

2. Unfold yardage and separate fabrics by color. To help reduce raveling, use scissors to snip a small triangle from each corner of your fabric pieces. Machine wash fabrics in warm water with a small amount of mild laundry detergent. Do not use fabric softener. Rinse well and then dry fabrics in the dryer, checking long fabric lengths occasionally to make sure they are not tangling.

3. To make ironing easier, remove fabrics from dryer while they are slightly damp. Refold each fabric lengthwise (as it was on the bolt) with wrong sides together and matching selvages. If necessary, adjust slightly at selvages so that fold lies flat. Press each fabric with a steam iron set on "Cotton."

ROTARY CUTTING

*Based on the idea that you can easily cut strips of fabric and then cut those strips into smaller pieces, rotary cutting has brought speed and accuracy to quiltmaking. Observe safety precautions when using the rotary cutter since it is extremely sharp. Develop a habit of retracting the blade guard **just before** making a cut and closing it **immediately afterward**, before laying down the cutter.*

1. Follow **Preparing Fabrics** to wash, dry, and press fabrics.

2. Cut all strips from the selvage-to-selvage width of the fabric unless otherwise indicated. Place fabric on the cutting mat as shown in **Fig. 1** with the fold of the fabric toward you. To straighten the uneven fabric edge, make the first "squaring up" cut by placing the right edge of the rotary cutting ruler over the left raw edge of the fabric. Place right-angle triangle (or another rotary cutting ruler) with the lower edge carefully aligned with the fold and the left edge against the ruler (**Fig. 1**). Hold the ruler firmly with your left hand, placing your little finger off the left edge to anchor the ruler. Remove the triangle, pick up the rotary cutter, and retract the blade guard. Using a smooth, downward motion, make the cut by running the blade of the rotary cutter firmly along the right edge of the ruler (**Fig. 2**). **Always** cut in a direction **away** from your body and **immediately** close the blade guard after each cut.

Fig. 1

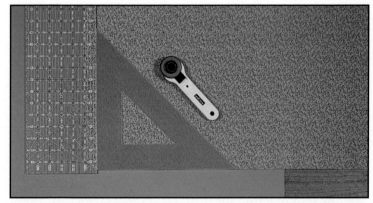

Fig. 2

3. To cut each of the strips required for the project, place the ruler over the cut edge of the fabric, aligning desired marking on the ruler with the cut edge (**Fig. 3**) and then make the cut. When cutting several strips from a single piece of fabric, it is important to occasionally use the ruler and triangle to ensure that cuts are still at a perfect right angle to the fold. If not, repeat Step 2 to straighten.

Fig. 3

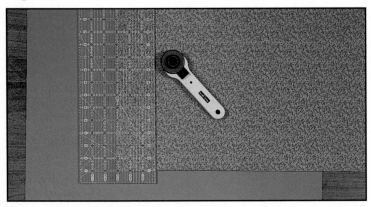

4. To square up selvage ends of a strip before cutting pieces, refer to **Fig. 4** and place folded strip on mat with selvage ends to your right. Aligning a horizontal marking on ruler with 1 long edge of strip, use rotary cutter to trim off selvage to make end of strip square and even (**Fig. 4**). Turn strip (or entire mat) so that cut end is to your left before making subsequent cuts.

Fig. 4

5. Pieces such as rectangles and squares can now be cut from strips. (Cutting other shapes such as diamonds is discussed in individual project instructions.) Usually strips remain folded, and pieces are cut in pairs after ends of strips are squared up. To cut squares or rectangles from a strip, place ruler over left end of strip, aligning desired marking on ruler with cut end of strip. To ensure perfectly square cuts, align a horizontal marking on ruler with 1 long edge of strip (**Fig. 5**) before making the cut.

Fig. 5

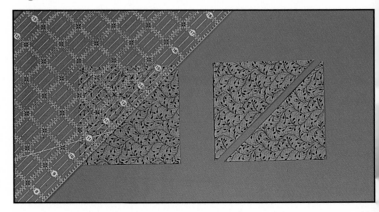

6. To cut 2 triangles from a square, cut square the size indicated in the project instructions. Cut square once diagonally to make 2 triangles (**Fig. 6**).

Fig. 6

7. To cut 4 triangles from a square, cut square the size indicated in the project instructions. Cut square twice diagonally to make 4 triangles (**Fig. 7**). You may find it helpful to use a small rotary cutting mat so that mat can be turned to make second cut without disturbing fabric pieces.

Fig. 7

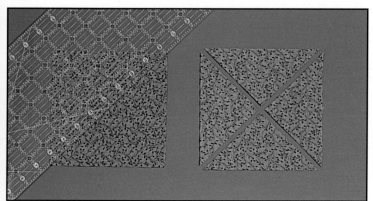

8. After some practice, you may want to try stacking up to 6 fabric layers when making cuts. When stacking strips, match long cut edges and follow Step 4 to square up ends of strip stack. Carefully turn stack (or entire mat) so that squared-up ends are to your left before making subsequent cuts. After cutting, check accuracy of pieces. Some shapes, such as diamonds, are more difficult to cut accurately in stacks.

9. In some cases, strips will be sewn together into strip sets before being cut into smaller units. When cutting a strip set, align a seam in strip set with a horizontal marking on the ruler to maintain square cuts (**Fig. 8**). We do not recommend stacking strip sets for rotary cutting.

Fig. 8

10. Most borders for quilts in this book are cut along the more stable lengthwise grain to minimize wavy edges caused by stretching. To remove selvages before cutting lengthwise strips, place fabric on mat with selvages to your left and squared-up end at bottom of mat. Placing ruler over selvage and using squared-up edge instead of fold, follow Step 2 to cut away selvages as you did raw edges (**Fig. 9**). After making a cut the length of the mat, move the next section of fabric to be cut onto the mat. Repeat until you have removed selvages from required length of fabric.

Fig. 9

11. After removing selvages, place ruler over left edge of fabric, aligning desired marking on ruler with cut edge of fabric. Make cuts as in Step 3. After each cut, move next section of fabric onto mat as in Step 10.

TEMPLATE CUTTING

Our full-sized piecing templates have 2 lines: a solid cutting line and a dashed line showing the ¹/₄" seam allowance.

1. To make a template from a pattern, use a permanent fine-point marker to carefully trace pattern onto template plastic, making sure to transfer all alignment and grain line markings. Cut out template along inner edge of drawn line. Check template against original pattern for accuracy.

2. To use a template, place template on wrong side of fabric, aligning grain line on template with straight grain of fabric. Use a sharp fabric marking pencil to draw around template. Transfer all alignment markings to fabric. Cut out fabric piece using scissors or rotary cutter and ruler.

PIECING AND PRESSING

Precise cutting, followed by accurate piecing and careful pressing, will ensure that all the pieces of your quilt top fit together well.

PIECING

Set sewing machine stitch length for approximately 11 stitches per inch. Use a new, sharp needle suited for medium-weight woven fabric.

Use a neutral-colored general-purpose sewing thread (not quilting thread) in the needle and in the bobbin. Stitch first on a scrap of fabric to check upper and bobbin thread tension; make any adjustments necessary.

For good results, it is **essential** that you stitch with an **accurate ¼" seam allowance**. On many sewing machines, the measurement from the needle to the outer edge of the presser foot is ¼". If this is the case with your machine, the presser foot is your best guide. If not, measure ¼" from the needle and mark with a piece of masking tape. Special presser feet that are exactly ¼" wide are also available for most sewing machines.

When piecing, **always** place pieces **right sides together** and **match raw edges**; pin if necessary. (If using straight pins, remove the pins just before they reach the sewing machine needle.)

Chain Piecing

Chain piecing whenever possible will make your work go faster and will usually result in more accurate piecing. Stack the pieces you will be sewing beside your machine in the order you will need them and in a position that will allow you to easily pick them up. Pick up each pair of pieces, carefully place them together as they will be sewn, and feed them into the machine one after the other. Stop between each pair only long enough to pick up the next and don't cut thread between pairs (**Fig. 10**). After all pieces are sewn, cut threads, press, and go on to the next step, chain piecing when possible.

Fig. 10

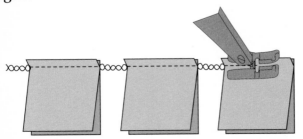

Sewing Strip Sets

When there are several strips to assemble into a strip set, first sew the strips together into pairs, then sew the pairs together to form the strip set. To help avoid distortion, sew 1 seam in 1 direction and then sew the next seam in the opposite direction (**Fig. 11**).

Fig. 11

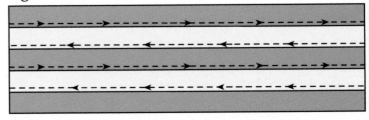

Sewing Across Seam Intersections

When sewing across the intersection of 2 seams, place pieces right sides together and match seams exactly, making sure seam allowances are pressed in opposite directions (**Fig. 12**). To prevent fabric from shifting, you may wish to pin in place.

Fig. 12

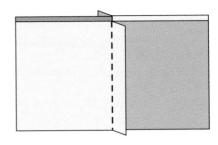

Sewing Sharp Points

To ensure sharp points when joining triangular or diagonal pieces, stitch across the center of the "X" (shown in pink) formed on the wrong side by previous seams (**Fig. 13**).

Fig. 13

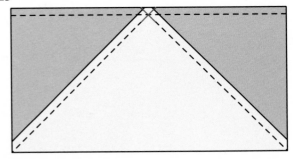

Sewing Bias Seams

Care should be used in handling and stitching bias edges, since they stretch easily. After sewing the seam, carefully press seam allowances to 1 side, making sure not to stretch the fabric.

Making Triangle-Squares

The grid method for making triangle-squares is faster and more accurate than cutting and sewing individual triangles. Stitching before cutting the triangle-squares apart also prevents stretching the bias edges.

1. Follow project instructions to cut rectangles or squares of fabric for making triangle-squares. Place the indicated pieces right sides together and press.
2. On the wrong side of the lighter fabric, draw a grid of squares similar to that shown in **Fig. 14**. The size and number of squares will be given in the project instructions.

Fig. 14

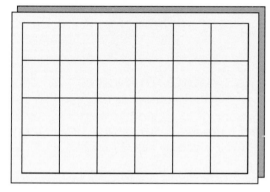

3. Following the example given in the project instructions, draw 1 diagonal line through each square in the grid (**Fig. 15**).

Fig. 15

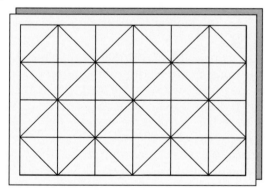

4. Stitch ¹/₄" on each side of all diagonal lines. For accuracy, it may be helpful to first draw your stitching lines onto the fabric, especially if your presser foot is not your ¹/₄" guide. In some cases, stitching may be done in a single continuous line. Project instructions include a diagram similar to **Fig. 16**, which shows stitching lines and the direction of the stitching.

Fig. 16

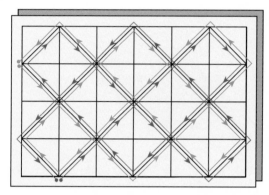

5. Use rotary cutter and ruler to cut along all drawn lines of the grid. Each square of the grid will yield 2 triangle-squares (**Fig. 17**).

Fig. 17

6. Carefully press triangle-squares open, pressing seam allowances toward darker fabric. Trim off points of seam allowances that extend beyond edges of triangle-square (see **Fig. 22**, page 84).

Working with Diamonds and Set-in Seams

Piecing diamonds and sewing set-in seams require special handling. For best results, carefully follow the steps below.

1. When sewing 2 diamond pieces together, place pieces right sides together, carefully matching edges; pin. Mark a small dot ¹/₄" from corner of 1 piece as shown in **Fig. 18**. Stitch pieces together in the direction shown, stopping at center of dot and backstitching.

Fig. 18

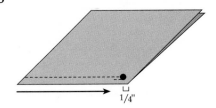

2. For best results, add side triangles, then corner squares to diamond sections. Mark corner of each piece to be set in with a small dot (**Fig. 19**).

Fig. 19

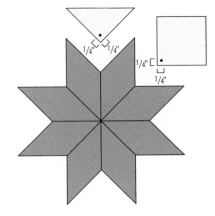

3. To sew first seam, match right sides and pin the triangle or square to the diamond on the left. Stitch seam from the outer edge to the dot, backstitching at the dot; clip threads (**Fig. 20**).

Fig. 20

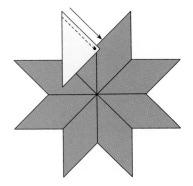

4. To sew the second seam, pivot the added triangle or square to match raw edges of next diamond. Beginning at dot, take 2 or 3 stitches, then backstitch, making sure not to backstitch into previous seam allowance. Continue stitching to outer edge (**Fig. 21**).

Fig. 21

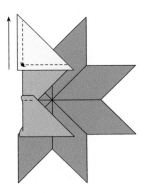

Trimming Seam Allowances

When sewing with diamond or triangle pieces, some seam allowances may extend beyond the edges of the sewn pieces. Trim away "dog ears" that extend beyond the edges of the sewn pieces (**Fig. 22**).

Fig. 22

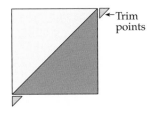

PRESSING

Use a steam iron set on "Cotton" for all pressing. Press as you sew, taking care to prevent small folds along seamlines. Seam allowances are almost always pressed to one side, usually toward the darker fabric. However, to reduce bulk it may occasionally be necessary to press seam allowances toward the lighter fabric or even to press them open. In order to prevent a dark fabric seam allowance from showing through a light fabric, trim the darker seam allowance slightly narrower than the lighter seam allowance. To press long seams, such as those in long strip sets, without curving or other distortion, lay strips across the width of the ironing board.

APPLIQUÉ

PREPARING FUSIBLE APPLIQUÉS

Patterns are printed in reverse to enable you to use our speedy method of preparing appliqués. White or light-colored fabrics may need to be lined with fusible interfacing before applying fusible web to prevent darker fabrics from showing through.

1. Place paper-backed fusible web, web side down, over appliqué pattern. Use a pencil to trace pattern onto paper side of web as many times as indicated in project instructions for a single fabric. Repeat for additional patterns and fabrics.
2. Follow manufacturer's instructions to fuse traced patterns to wrong side of fabrics. Do not remove paper backing.
3. Some projects may have pieces that are given as measurements (such as a 2" x 4" rectangle) instead of drawn patterns. Fuse web to wrong side of the fabrics indicated for these pieces.
4. Use scissors to cut out appliqué pieces along traced lines; use rotary cutting equipment to cut out appliqué pieces given as measurements. Remove paper backing from all pieces.

INVISIBLE APPLIQUÉ

This method of appliqué is an adaptation of satin stitch appliqué that uses clear nylon thread to secure the appliqué pieces. Transparent monofilament (clear nylon) thread is available in 2 colors: clear and smoke. Use clear on white or very light fabrics and smoke on darker colors.

1. Referring to diagram and/or photo, arrange appliqués on the background fabric and follow manufacturer's instructions to fuse in place.
2. Pin a stabilizer, such as paper or any of the commercially available products, on wrong side of background fabric before stitching appliqués in place.
3. Thread sewing machine with transparent monofilament thread; use general-purpose thread that matches background fabric in bobbin.
4. Set sewing machine for a very narrow (approximately $^1/_{16}$") zigzag stitch and a short stitch length. You may find that loosening the top tension slightly will yield a smoother stitch.
5. Begin by stitching 2 or 3 stitches in place (drop feed dogs or set stitch length at 0) to anchor thread. Most of the zigzag stitch should be done on the appliqué with the right edges of the stitch falling at the very outside edge of the appliqué. Stitch over all exposed raw edges of appliqué pieces.

6. (*Note:* Dots on **Figs. 23 - 28** indicate where to leave needle in fabric when pivoting.) For **outside corners**, stitch just past the corner, stopping with the needle in **background** fabric (**Fig. 23**). Raise presser foot. Pivot project, lower presser foot, and stitch adjacent side (**Fig. 24**).

Fig. 23   **Fig. 24**

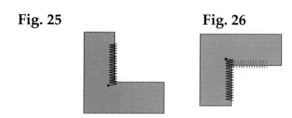

7. For **inside corners**, stitch just past the corner, stopping with the needle in **appliqué** fabric (**Fig. 25**). Raise presser foot. Pivot project, lower presser foot, and stitch adjacent side (**Fig. 26**).

Fig. 25   **Fig. 26**

8. When stitching **outside** curves, stop with needle in **background** fabric. Raise presser foot and pivot project as needed. Lower presser foot and continue stitching, pivoting as often as necessary to follow curve (**Fig. 27**).

Fig. 27

9. When stitching **inside** curves, stop with needle in **appliqué** fabric. Raise presser foot and pivot project as needed. Lower presser foot and continue stitching, pivoting as often as necessary to follow curve (**Fig. 28**).

Fig. 28

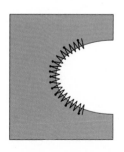

10. Do not backstitch at end of stitching. Pull threads to wrong side of background fabric; knot thread and trim ends.
11. Carefully tear away stabilizer.

BORDERS

Borders cut along the lengthwise grain will lie flatter than borders cut along the crosswise grain. In most cases, our instructions for cutting borders for bed-size quilts include an extra 2" of length at each end for "insurance"; borders will be trimmed after measuring completed center section of quilt top.

ADDING SQUARED BORDERS

1. Mark the center of each edge of quilt top.
2. Squared borders are usually added to top and bottom, then side edges of the center section of a quilt top. To add top and bottom borders, measure across center of quilt top to determine length of borders (**Fig. 29**). Trim top and bottom borders to the determined length.

Fig. 29

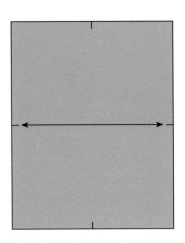

3. Mark center of 1 long edge of top border. Matching center marks and raw edges, pin border to quilt top, easing in any fullness; stitch. Repeat for bottom border.
4. Measure center of quilt top, including attached borders, to determine length of side borders. Trim side borders to the determined length. Repeat Step 3 to add borders to quilt top (**Fig. 30**).

Fig. 30

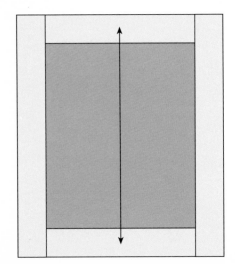

ADDING MITERED BORDERS

1. Mark the center of each edge of quilt top.
2. Mark center of 1 long edge of top border. Measure across center of quilt top (see **Fig. 29**). Matching center marks and raw edges, pin border to center of quilt top edge. Beginning at center of border, measure $1/2$ the width of the quilt top in both directions and mark. Match marks on border with corners of quilt top and pin. Easing in any fullness, pin border to quilt top between center and corners. Sew border to quilt top, beginning and ending seams **exactly** $1/4$" from each corner of quilt top and backstitching at beginning and end of stitching (**Fig. 31**).

Fig. 31

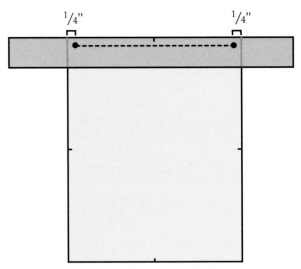

3. Repeat Step 2 to sew bottom, then side borders, to center section of quilt top. To temporarily move first 2 borders out of the way, fold and pin ends as shown in **Fig. 32**.

Fig. 32

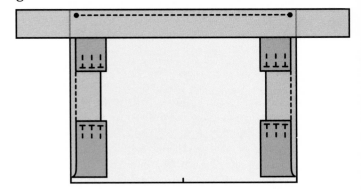

4. Fold 1 corner of quilt top diagonally with right sides together and matching edges. Use ruler to mark stitching line as shown in **Fig. 33**. Pin borders together along drawn line. Sew on drawn line, backstitching at beginning and end of stitching (**Fig. 34**).

Fig. 33

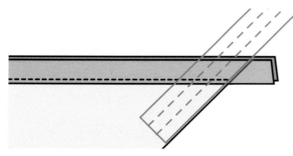

Fig. 34

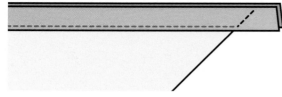

5. Turn mitered corner right side up. Check to make sure corner will lie flat with no gaps or puckers.
6. Trim seam allowance to $^1/_4$"; press to 1 side.
7. Repeat Steps 4 - 6 to miter each remaining corner.

QUILTING

Quilting holds the 3 layers (top, batting, and backing) of the quilt together and can be done by hand or machine. Our project instructions tell you which method is used on each project and show you quilting diagrams that can be used as suggestions for marking quilting designs. Because marking, layering, and quilting are interrelated and may be done in different orders depending on circumstances, please read this entire section, pages 87 - 91, before beginning the quilting process on your project.

TYPES OF QUILTING
In the Ditch
Quilting very close to a seamline (**Fig. 35**) or appliqué (**Fig. 36**) is called "in the ditch" quilting. This type of quilting does not need to be marked and is indicated on our quilting diagrams with blue lines close to seamlines. When quilting in the ditch, quilt on the side **opposite** the seam allowance.

Fig. 35

Fig. 36

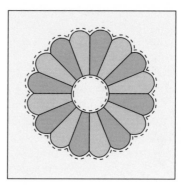

Outline Quilting
Quilting approximately $^1/_4$" from a seam or appliqué is called "outline" quilting (**Fig. 37**). This type of quilting is indicated on our quilting diagrams by blue lines a short distance from seamlines. Outline quilting may be marked, or you may place $^1/_4$"w masking tape along seamlines and quilt along the opposite edge of the tape. (Do not leave tape on quilt longer than necessary, since it may leave an adhesive residue.)

Fig. 37

Ornamental Quilting

Quilting decorative lines or designs is called "ornamental" quilting (**Fig. 38**). Ornamental quilting is indicated on our quilting diagrams by blue lines. This type of quilting should be marked before you baste quilt layers together.

Fig. 38

MARKING QUILTING LINES

Fabric marking pencils, various types of chalk markers, and fabric marking pens with inks that disappear with exposure to air or water are readily available and work well for different applications. Lead pencils work well on light-colored fabric, but marks may be difficult to remove. White pencils work well on dark-colored fabric, and silver pencils show up well on many colors. Since chalk rubs off easily, it's a good choice if you are marking as you quilt. Fabric marking pens make more durable and visible markings, but the marks should be carefully removed according to manufacturer's instructions. Press down only as hard as necessary to make a visible line.

When you choose to mark your quilt, whether before or after the layers are basted together, is also a factor in deciding which marking tool to use. If you mark with chalk or a chalk pencil, handling the quilt during basting may rub off the markings. Intricate or ornamental designs may not be practical to mark as you quilt; mark these designs before basting using a more durable marker.

To choose marking tools, take all these factors into consideration and **test** different markers **on scrap fabric** until you find the one that gives the desired result.

USING QUILTING STENCILS

A wide variety of pre-cut quilting stencils, as well as entire books of quilting patterns, are available at your local quilt shop or fabric store. Wherever you draw your quilting inspiration from, using a stencil makes it easier to mark intricate or repetitive designs on your quilt top.

1. To make a stencil from a pattern, center template plastic over pattern and use a permanent marker to trace pattern onto plastic.
2. Use a craft knife with a single or double blade to cut narrow slits along traced lines (**Fig. 39**).

Fig. 39

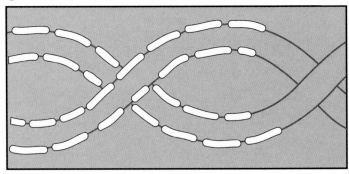

3. Use desired marking tool and stencil to mark quilting lines.

CHOOSING AND PREPARING THE BACKING

To allow for slight shifting of the quilt top during quilting, the backing should be approximately 4" larger on all sides for a bed-size quilt top. Yardage requirements listed for quilt backings are calculated for 45"w fabric. If you are making a bed-size quilt, using 90"w or 108"w fabric for the backing may eliminate piecing. To piece a backing using 45"w fabric, use the following instructions.

1. Measure length and width of quilt top; add 8" to each measurement.
2. If quilt top is 76"w or less, cut backing fabric into 2 lengths slightly longer than the determined **length** measurement. Trim selvages. Place lengths with right sides facing and sew long edges together, forming a tube (**Fig. 40**).

Fig. 40

3. Match seams and press along 1 fold (**Fig. 41**).

Fig. 41

4. Cut along pressed fold to form a single piece (**Fig. 42**).

Fig. 42

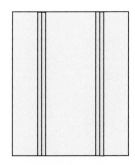

5. If quilt top is more than 76"w, cut backing fabric into 3 lengths slightly longer than the determined **width** measurement. Trim selvages. Sew long edges together to form a single piece.

6. Trim backing to correct size, if necessary, and press seam allowances open.

CHOOSING AND PREPARING THE BATTING

Choosing the right batting will make your quilting job easier. For fine hand quilting, choose a low-loft batting in any of the fiber types described here. Machine quilters will want to choose a low-loft batting that is all cotton or a cotton/polyester blend because the cotton helps "grip" the layers of the quilt. If the quilt is to be tied, a high-loft batting, sometimes called extra-loft or fat batting, is a good choice.

Batting is available in many different fibers. Bonded polyester batting is one of the most popular batting types. It is treated with a protective coating to stabilize the fibers and to reduce "bearding," a process where batting fibers work their way out through the quilt fabrics. Other batting options include cotton/polyester batting, which combines the best of both polyester and cotton battings; all-cotton batting, which must be quilted more closely than polyester batting; and wool and silk battings, which are generally more expensive and are usually only dry-cleanable.

Whichever batting you choose, read the manufacturer's instructions closely for any special notes on care or preparation. When you're ready to use your chosen batting in a project, cut the batting the same size as the prepared backing.

LAYERING THE QUILT

1. Examine wrong side of quilt top closely; trim any seam allowances and clip any threads that may show through the front of the quilt. Press quilt top.

2. If quilt top is to be marked before layering, mark quilting lines (see **Marking Quilting Lines**, page 88).

3. Place backing **wrong** side up on a flat surface. Use masking tape to tape edges of backing to surface. Place batting on top of backing fabric. Smooth batting gently, being careful not to stretch or tear. Center quilt top **right** side up on batting.

4. If hand quilting, begin in the center and work toward the outer edges to hand baste all layers together. Use long stitches and place basting lines approximately 4" apart (**Fig. 43**). Smooth fullness or wrinkles toward outer edges.

Fig. 43

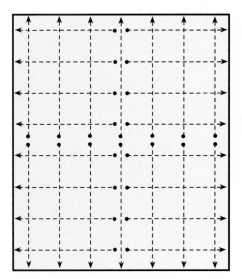

5. If machine quilting, use 1" rust-proof safety pins to "pin-baste" all layers together, spacing pins approximately 4" apart. Begin at the center and work toward the outer edges to secure all layers. If possible, place pins away from areas that will be quilted, although pins may be removed as needed when quilting.

HAND QUILTING

The quilting stitch is a basic running stitch that forms a broken line on the quilt top and backing. Stitches on the quilt top and backing should be straight and equal in length.

1. Secure center of quilt in hoop or frame. Check quilt top and backing to make sure they are smooth. To help prevent puckers, always begin quilting in the center of the quilt and work toward the outside edges.
2. Thread needle with an 18" - 20" length of quilting thread; knot 1 end. Using a thimble, insert needle into quilt top and batting approximately $1/2$" from where you wish to begin quilting. Bring needle up at the point where you wish to begin (**Fig. 44**); when knot catches on quilt top, give thread a quick, short pull to "pop" knot through fabric into batting (**Fig. 45**).

Fig. 44

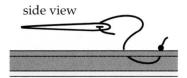

Fig. 45

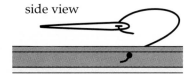

3. Holding the needle with your sewing hand and placing your other hand underneath the quilt, use thimble to push the tip of the needle down through all layers. As soon as needle touches your finger underneath, use that finger to push the tip of the needle only back up through the layers to top of quilt. (The amount of the needle showing above the fabric determines the length of the quilting stitch.) Referring to **Fig. 46**, rock the needle up and down, taking 3 - 6 stitches before bringing the needle and thread completely through the layers. Check the back of the quilt to make sure stitches are going through all layers. When quilting through a seam allowance or quilting a curve or corner, you may need to take 1 stitch at a time.

Fig. 46

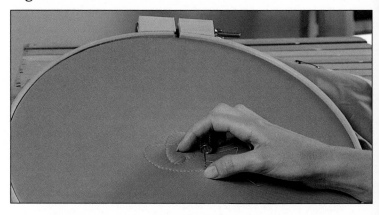

4. When you reach the end of your thread, knot thread close to the fabric and "pop" knot into batting; clip thread close to fabric.
5. Stop and move your hoop as often as necessary. You do not have to tie a knot every time you move your hoop; you may leave the thread dangling and pick it up again when you return to that part of the quilt.

MACHINE QUILTING

The machine-quilted projects in this book feature straight-line quilting, which requires a walking foot or even-feed foot. The term "straight-line" is somewhat deceptive, since curves (especially gentle ones) as well as straight lines can be stitched with this technique.

1. Wind your sewing machine bobbin with general-purpose thread that matches the quilt backing. Do not use quilting thread. Thread the needle of your machine with transparent monofilament thread if you want your quilting to blend with your quilt top fabrics. Use decorative thread, such as a metallic or contrasting-colored general-purpose thread, when you want the quilting lines to stand out more. Set the stitch length for 6 - 10 stitches per inch and attach the walking foot to sewing machine.

2. After pin-basting, decide which section of the quilt will have the longest continuous quilting line, oftentimes the area from center top to center bottom. Leaving the area exposed where you will place your first line of quilting, roll up each edge of the quilt to help reduce the bulk, keeping fabrics smooth. Smaller projects may not need to be rolled.

3. Start stitching at beginning of longest quilting line, using very short stitches for the first $1/4$" to "lock" beginning of quilting line. Stitch across project, using one hand on each side of the walking foot to slightly spread the fabric and to guide the fabric through the machine. Lock stitches at end of quilting line.

4. Continue machine quilting, stitching the longer quilting lines first to stabilize the quilt before moving on to other areas.

TYING A QUILT

Tied quilts use yarn or floss ties instead of quilting stitches to secure the layers. For a tied quilt, be sure to use bonded batting to prevent separation or bunching when the quilt is laundered. You may also use a higher loft batting than when quilting.

1. Determine where ties will be placed and mark if necessary. Space ties evenly. On a pieced top, tie at corners of blocks or pieces within blocks.

2. Follow **Layering the Quilt**, page 89, to prepare quilt for tying.

3. Thread a large darning needle with a long length of embroidery floss, yarn, or pearl cotton; do not knot.

4. At each mark or tie location, take a small stitch through all layers of quilt. Pull up floss, but do not cut between stitches (**Fig. 47**). Begin at center of quilt and work toward outside edges, rethreading needle as necessary.

Fig. 47

5. Cut floss between stitches. At each stitch, use a square knot to tie floss securely (**Fig. 48**); trim ties to desired length.

Fig. 48

BINDING

Binding encloses the raw edges of your quilt. Because of its stretchiness, bias binding works well for binding projects with curves or rounded corners and tends to lie smooth and flat in any given circumstance. It is also more durable than other types of binding. Binding may also be cut from the straight lengthwise or crosswise grain of the fabric. You will find that straight-grain binding works well for projects with straight edges.

MAKING CONTINUOUS BIAS STRIP BINDING

Bias strips for binding can simply be cut and pieced to the desired length. However, when a long length of binding is needed, the "continuous" method is quick and accurate.

1. Cut a square from binding fabric the size indicated in the project instructions. Cut square in half diagonally to make 2 triangles.

2. With right sides together and using a $1/4$" seam allowance, sew triangles together (**Fig. 49**); press seam allowance open.

Fig. 49

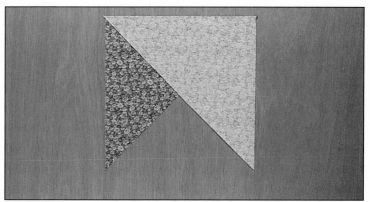

3. On wrong side of fabric, draw lines the width of the binding as specified in the project instructions, usually $2\frac{1}{2}$" (**Fig. 50**). Cut off any remaining fabric less than this width.

Fig. 50

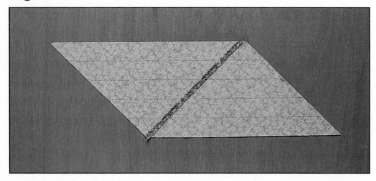

4. With right sides inside, bring short edges together to form a tube; match raw edges so that first drawn line of top section meets second drawn line of bottom section (**Fig. 51**).

Fig. 51

5. Carefully pin edges together by inserting pins through drawn lines at the point where drawn lines intersect, making sure the pins go through intersections on both sides. Using a $\frac{1}{4}$" seam allowance, sew edges together. Press seam allowance open.

6. To cut continuous strip, begin cutting along first drawn line (**Fig. 52**). Continue cutting along drawn line around tube.

Fig. 52

7. Trim ends of bias strip square.
8. Matching wrong sides and raw edges, press bias strip in half lengthwise to complete binding.

MAKING STRAIGHT-GRAIN BINDING

1. To determine length of strip needed if attaching binding with mitered corners, measure edges of the quilt and add 12".
2. To determine lengths of strips needed if attaching binding with overlapped corners, measure each edge of quilt; add 3" to each measurement.
3. Cut lengthwise or crosswise strips of binding fabric the determined length and the width called for in the project instructions. Strips may be pieced to achieve the necessary length.
4. Matching wrong sides and raw edges, press strip(s) in half lengthwise to complete binding.

ATTACHING BINDING WITH MITERED CORNERS

1. Press 1 end of binding diagonally (**Fig. 53**).

Fig. 53

2. Lay binding around quilt to make sure that seams in binding will not end up at a corner. Adjust placement if necessary. Matching raw edges of binding to raw edge of quilt top and beginning with pressed end several inches from a corner, pin binding to right side of quilt along 1 edge.
3. When you reach the first corner, mark $\frac{1}{4}$" from corner of quilt top (**Fig. 54**).

Fig. 54

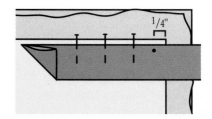

4. Using a $\frac{1}{4}$" seam allowance, sew binding to quilt, backstitching at beginning of stitching and when you reach the mark (**Fig. 55**). Lift needle out of fabric and clip thread.

Fig. 55

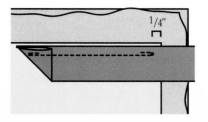

5. Fold binding as shown in **Figs. 56** and **57** and pin binding to adjacent side, matching raw edges. When you reach the next corner, mark $1/4$" from edge of quilt top.

Fig. 56

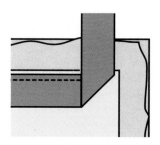

Fig. 57

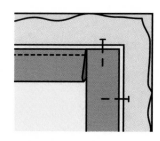

6. Backstitching at edge of quilt top, sew pinned binding to quilt (**Fig. 58**); backstitch when you reach the next mark. Lift needle out of fabric and clip thread.

Fig. 58

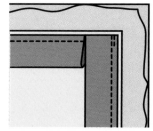

7. Repeat Steps 5 and 6 to continue sewing binding to quilt until binding overlaps beginning end by approximately 2". Trim excess binding.

8. Trim backing and batting a scant $1/4$" larger than quilt top so that batting and backing will fill the binding when it is folded over to the quilt backing.

9. On 1 edge of quilt, fold binding over to quilt backing and pin pressed edge in place, covering stitching line (**Fig. 59**). On adjacent side, fold binding over, forming a mitered corner (**Fig. 60**). Repeat to pin remainder of binding in place.

Fig. 59   **Fig. 60**

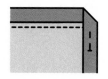

10. Blindstitch binding to backing, taking care not to stitch through to front of quilt.

ATTACHING BINDING WITH OVERLAPPED CORNERS

1. Matching raw edges and using a $1/4$" seam allowance, sew a length of binding to top and bottom edges on right side of quilt.

2. Trim backing and batting from top and bottom edges a scant $1/4$" larger than quilt top so that batting and backing will fill the binding when it is folded over to the quilt backing.

3. Trim ends of top and bottom binding even with edges of quilt top. Fold binding over to quilt backing and pin pressed edges in place, covering stitching line (**Fig. 61**); blindstitch binding to backing.

Fig. 61

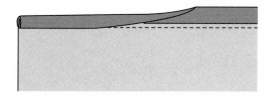

4. Leaving approximately $1^{1}/2$" of binding at each end, stitch a length of binding to each side edge of quilt. Trim backing and batting as in Step 2.

5. Trim each end of binding $1/2$" longer than bound edge. Fold each end of binding over to quilt backing (**Fig. 62**); pin in place. Fold binding over to quilt backing and blindstitch in place, taking care not to stitch through to front of quilt.

Fig. 62

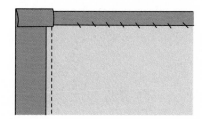

SIGNING AND DATING YOUR QUILT

Your completed quilt is a work of art and should be treated as such. And like any artist, you should sign and date your work. There are many different ways to do this, and you should pick a method of signing and dating that reflects the style of the quilt, the occasion for which it was made, and your own particular talents.

The following suggestions may give you an idea for recording the history of your quilt for future generations.

- Embroider your name, the date, and any additional information on the quilt top or backing. You may choose floss colors that closely match the fabric you are working on, such as white floss on a white border, or contrasting colors may be used.
- Make a label from muslin and use a permanent marker to write your information. Your label may be as plain or as fancy as you wish. Then stitch the label to the back of the quilt.
- Chart a cross-stitch label design that includes the information you wish and stitch it in colors that complement the quilt. Stitch the finished label to the quilt backing.

GLOSSARY

Appliqué — A cutout fabric shape that is secured to a larger background. Also refers to the technique of securing the cutout pieces.

Backing — The back or bottom layer of a quilt, sometimes called the "lining."

Backstitch — A reinforcing stitch taken at the beginning and end of a seam to secure stitches.

Basting — Large running stitches used to temporarily secure pieces or layers of fabric together. Basting is removed after permanent stitching.

Batting — The middle layer of a quilt that provides the insulation and warmth as well as the thickness.

Bias — The diagonal (45° for true bias) grain of fabric in relation to crosswise or lengthwise grain (see **Fig. 63**).

Binding — The fabric strip used to enclose the raw edges of the layered and quilted quilt. Also refers to the technique of finishing quilt edges in this way.

Blindstitch — A method of hand sewing an opening closed so that it is invisible.

Border — Strips of fabric that are used to frame a quilt top.

Chain piecing — A machine-piecing method consisting of joining pairs of pieces one after the other by feeding them through the sewing machine without cutting the thread between the pairs.

Grain — The direction of the threads in woven fabric. "Crosswise grain" refers to the threads running from selvage to selvage. "Lengthwise grain" refers to the threads running parallel to the selvages (**Fig. 63**).

Fig. 63

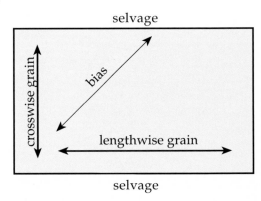

Machine baste — To baste using a sewing machine set at a long stitch length.

Miter — A method used to finish corners of quilt borders or bindings consisting of joining fabric pieces at a 45° angle.

Piecing — Sewing together the pieces of a quilt design to form a quilt block or an entire quilt top.

Pin basting — Using rust-proof safety pins to secure the layers of a quilt together prior to machine quilting.

Quilt block — Pieced or appliquéd sections that are sewn together to form a quilt top.

Quilt top — The decorative part of a quilt that is layered on top of the batting and backing.

Quilting — The stitching that holds together the 3 quilt layers (top, batting, and backing); or, the entire process of making a quilt.

Running stitch — A series of straight stitches with the stitch length equal to the space between stitches (**Fig. 64**).

Fig. 64

Sashing — Strips or blocks of fabric that separate individual blocks in a quilt top.

Seam allowance — The distance between the seam and the cut edge of the fabric. In quilting, the seam allowance is usually $\frac{1}{4}$".

Selvages — The 2 finished lengthwise edges of fabric (see **Fig. 63**). Selvages should be trimmed from fabric before cutting.

Set (or Setting) — The arrangement of the quilt blocks as they are sewn together to form the quilt top.

Setting squares — Squares of plain (unpieced) fabric set between pieced or appliquéd quilt blocks in a quilt top.

Setting triangles — Triangles of fabric used around the outside of a diagonally-set quilt top to fill in between outer squares and border or binding.

Stencil — A pattern used for marking quilting lines.

Straight grain — The crosswise or lengthwise grain of fabric (see **Fig. 63**). The lengthwise grain has the least amount of stretch.

Strip set — Two or more strips of fabric that are sewn together along the long edges and then cut apart across the width of the sewn strips to create smaller units.

Template — A pattern used for marking quilt pieces to be cut out.

Triangle-square — In piecing, 2 right triangles joined along their long sides to form a square with a diagonal seam (**Fig. 65**).

Fig. 65

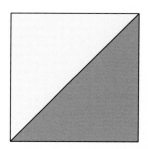

Unit— A pieced section that is made as individual steps in the quilt construction process are completed. Units are usually combined to make blocks or other sections of the quilt top.